KAMALA DAS

A CRITICAL SPECTRUM

KAMALA DAS

A CRITICAL SPECTRUM

Edited by

RAJESHWAR MITTAPALLI
PIER PAOLO PICIUCCO

PUBLISHERS & DISTRIBUTORS (P) LTD

Published by

ATLANTIC

PUBLISHERS & DISTRIBUTORS (P) LTD

7/22, Ansari Road, Darya Ganj,
New Delhi-110002
Phones : +91-11-40775252, 23273880, 23275880, 23280451
Fax : +91-11-23285873
Web : www.atlanticbooks.com
E-mail : orders@atlanticbooks.com

Branch Office
5, Nallathambi Street, Wallajah Road,
Chennai-600002
Phones : +91-44-64611085, 32413319
E-mail : chennai@atlanticbooks.com

Printed in India at Nice Printing Press, A-33/3A, Site-IV, Industrial Area, Sahibabad, Ghaziabad, U.P.

PREFACE

Kamala Das has been a unique literary phenomenon in India. Frank, bold and controversial in life and literature, Kamla Das made enormous contribution to the growth of Indian poetry in English. Although she sporadically ventured into the realms of fiction, she will be remembered primarily for her poetry because it is as a poet that she excels herself.

Her autobiography *My Story* raised a storm when it was first published more than two decades ago. It gave a rude jolt to the complacent and conformity ridden Indian society and its patriarchal values. The explicitness and honesty with which she admitted her feelings rattled many conservative minds. But perhaps the tradition of self-assertion and boldness can be traced to her broadly matrilineal heritage.

It is now agreed that her novels do not add to her image as a great literary personage. As a poet, however, Kamala Das indubitably merits a place beside the very best women poets of the twentieth century. She writes poetry as only a woman can write. She celebrates femininity, woman's body to be more specific, and in the process proves herself to be a feminist of the most radical kind. Her celebration of woman's body has not been taken kindly to by the conservative circles. However with growing sensitivity to the feelings of women and increasing stress being laid on the integrity of woman's body, in the intellectual, literary and social spheres in recent years, her poetry has come to be seen in an entirely different light. This understanding is reflected in the present volume which sets out to take a critical stock of the poetry of Kamla Das, often by bringing the understanding of feminist and other theories to bear upon it.

Kamala Das being a professed confessional poet, it is imperative that her life and poetry should be studied together. The articles on

My Story in this volume therefore set the tone by providing some crucial insights into her life and poetry. The other articles focus on various themes of her poetry such as love, nature, rebellion, split self, suffering, sex and feminism. At least two of the articles stress on the need to assess and reassess her poetry and that is what basically the bulk of the articles in this volume do.

We are grateful to all the contributors who promptly responded to our call for papers and to Dr. K.R. Gupta of Atlantic Publishers and Distributors who made the whole venture possible in the first place.

—EDITORS

CONTENTS

1

One Woman's Autobiography : Kamala Das's *My Story*

USHA V.T.*

As early as 1949, Simone de Beauvoir in *The Second Sex* wrote :

> Women do not set themselves up as subject and hence have erected to virile myth in which their projects are reflected; they have no religion or poetry of their own : they still dream through the dreams of men.

What Simone de Beauvoir said in 1949 in a language which might with some reservations be termed masculine seems still relevant, though perhaps not to the same extent, for the present time. Since then Feminist criticisms have taken several directions, but the need for the woman writer to express herself is foregrounded by major critics. In their Introduction to a collection of Feminist essays published in 1987 Gail Chester and Sigrid Nielson declare :

> Writing plays a vital part in forming our perceptions of our lives as women, in working out our feminist views and in communicating them to others.

Only by writing an expression could the woman writer succeed in breaking down existing social power structures and create a place for herself in the world of masculine hierarchies. The woman writer could thereby alter her existing marginalized position and accept her rightful role as a significant part of society. By writing the self,

*Department of English, University College, Trivandrum.

the woman writer could challenge accepted notions of the female and redraft general opinion on the feminine mystique. This exaggerated role of the woman writer is emphasized by another feminist writer Rosalind Brackenbury :

> Nobody writes in a vacuum, away from the political and social structures in which we live. We breathe the air of today's thought, we digest it in everything we read and consider; also, we create it. This is largely the role of women today: to create, present and consider a new world.

As the emphasis on demystifying the myth of the female and generating a new role for the woman in society became popular and more women writing began appear in public. The feeling of social responsibility in reconstructing her social role gave the woman writer courage and confidence. Freudian psychoanalysis where the verbalization of individual experience was considered therapeutic, made the autobiographical mode itself popular, the idea of autobiography as expression became an accepted means for the woman writer to explore her personal identity as well as create a newer and better perception on gender issues. Yet, by the very act of writing, the woman writer was constructed to be breaking social mores due to the valorization of silence as a desirable "feminine" attribute. By verbalizing, the woman writer was attempting a breaking up of the power structures of a hitherto acceptable patriarchal discourse. Linda Anderson theorizes upon this aspect of women's autobiographical discourse.

> It is necessary to take into account the fact that the woman who attempts to write herself is engaged by the very nature of that activity itself in rewriting the stories that already exist about her since by seeking to publicize herself she is violating an important cultural construction of her feminity as passive or hidden. She is resisting or changing what is known about her. Her place within culture, the place from which she writes, is produced by difference and produces differences.

The binary oppositions engendered by a woman writer's

autobiography call for a decentering of the thus for accepted phallocentric schemata. Her hesitant confessions or representations are dubbed subversive and by extension become controversial, creating a mental block in the hithertofore accepting readership. Her "otherness" is exaggerated making her seem an exception rather than a mouthpiece of the female community.

As a case in point, let us examine Kamala Das's once controversial autobiography *My Story*. It was marketed as "The compelling autobiography of the most controversial Indian writer." Reviewers viewed the work as one that would appeal to the male gaze and tickle their sensations :

> "The chapter headings accentuate the Excitement"
> ....There is enough in it to give...readers
> the "sizzle" and "spice"... .
>
> *(The Times of India)*
>
> *My Story* describes a life of frolicking on sex...
> The book has its accent on titillation...
>
> *(World Literature Today)*

Few saw the work as a woman's tale of woe, or paid heed to its themes of loneliness and subaltern anguish. Here, we can see how by the very act of defining female space, she was recognized as a threat to the adherents of patriarchal discourse. Severe critical dissent and adverse publicity followed suit and the writer had to withdraw into herself as a consequence.

The very qualities of forthrightness and expressiveness which would have been lauded in a male writer are pinpointed as her drawback. Thus, the writer who had attempted to define female space becomes different and unsure of her intrinsic worth. She feels compelled to provide an explanation for her work. In her Preface to *My Story*, Kamala Das explains her reasons for writing thus :

> The doctor thought that writing would distract my mind from the fear of a sudden death, and besides there were all the hospital bills to be taken care of.

Her insecurity in this role as well as her fear of the accompanying social disgrace make her cringe in embarrassment. Yet, despite the public outcry and social disparagement that the writer encountered, she enjoys the fulfilment that the creative activity involves for she states emphatically and quite rebelliously :

> This book has cost me many things that I held dear, but I do not for a moment regret having written it. I have written several books in my lifetime, but none of them provided the pleasure the writing of *My Story* has given me.

The tone of sincerity and the open confession of creative fulfilment in the writer's words underscore my point. The female autobiographist is viewed as radical and subversive when she writes the self and hence the diffidence and confusion that attends women's writing.

Notwithstanding the above, there are two other factors that are often brought up to demean the woman autobiographist — (1) autobiography as mere personal hysteria supported by Freud, and (2) autobiography as a fictional construct. Kamala Das, the autobiographer caters to both these factors and thereby lays herself open to criticism. She projects herself as the passive female, incapable of action and relapses into hysteria when the milieu becomes intolerable for her. When confronted with her husband's adultery and the illness of her son, for instance, she describes her state of mind thus :

> The growing misery inside me, the darkness that lay congealed removed from my face all that was once pretty. I was like a house with its lights put out. I walked up, up and down in our rooms wearing a torn saree and although my legs ached for rest, the movement went on and on as if they were propelled by some evil power (p. 103).

Despite the emphasis on autobiography and the aspects of personal confusion by Kamala Das, one is also aware of the work's fictional element. The very title itself — *My Story* — gives us an indication of the fictional aspect of the work. This is well in keeping with psychoanalytic theories of autobiography. They emphasize the in-consistencies achieved by selective retention during memorizing. Hence, the autobiographical narrative runs the risk of becoming merely a piece of fictional construction, quite at variance with the biography of the individual concerned. As James Olney explains,

> In the act of remembering the past in the present the autobiographer imagines into existence another world and surely it is *not* the same, in any real sense, as that past world that does not, under any circumstances, nor however much we may wish it now exist.

The above factor of fictionalization and/or glorification is one that is common to all autobiography and not merely women's autobiography. The possibility of distortion and/or exaggeration of self cannot be discounted.

But what strikes one as relevant is the element of universality in women's writing which cannot be sidetracked. By universality, I mean the collective repository of woman's experience that would ordinarily be marginalized and treated as superfluous. By writing the self the woman writer externalizes her inner experience and thereby subverts patriarchal stereotypes. Gail Chester and Sigrid Nielson explain the process thus :

> We may not have identical experience, but that does not mean we cannot share our different experiences. In writing for other women, we reinterpret our own experience in a way which brings us closer together. And women's experience is not only the sum total of each woman's memories, but a collective possession, a tradition which shapes the way we view our individual lives.

Thus, the sum total of the personal experiences of one individual expressed through her autobiography becomes a part of the repository of the universalized experience of womanhood. This is not to discount the plurality of the female sensibility or the variety and versatility of individual female identity. Despite the uniqueness and individuality of each woman's personal preoccupations, there is a common ground upon which women could share their views and express their opinions, whether good or bad.

Yet there are dangers inherent in the mere exploration of the female self. As part of the process of redefining the self and accentuating the difference/uniqueness of the female, the woman writer often explores her body as well as the biological sensations in sexual terms. In practice, this aspect is usually exploited by unscrupulous promoters and publishers of women's writing is undercut and misrepresented. Luce Irigaray, the noted feminist psychoanalyst warns against highlighting of the woman's biological essentialism :

> It is legitimate to expose the oppression, the mutilation, the 'functionalization' and the 'objectivation' of the female body, but it is also dangerous to put the female body at the centre of a search for female identity.

When the female body is exposed at length, there is the risk of other factors of female identity becoming sidetracked or ignored completely. For instance Kamala Das's *My Story* has been subjected to such phallocentric criticism and marketed as a saleable commodity.

Feminists confronted this problem by drawing up new terms of reference and an entirely different structural framework for woman writing. They called for a new language that would assist in expressing the female experience as such. Elaine Showalter explains the programme thus :

> The program of gynocritics is to construct a female framework for the analysis of women's literature, to develop new models based on the study of female experience, rather than adapt male models and theories.

A decentring of patriarchal power structures and reordering of the language of hierarchy to include the marginalized categories of experience is what the woman writer tries to achieve.

In all this discussion of the common female experience, what one tends to overlook is the plurality of the female experience. Through women all the world could relate experiences of a similar kind — tales of victimization, agony, exploitation, disgrace and abuse — what cannot be overlooked is the innate individuality and uniqueness of every person's experience. As Hiline Cixons explains,

> You can't talk about *a* female sexuality, homogeneous, classifiable into codes — any more

> than you can talk about one unconscious resembling another. Women's imaginary is inexhaustible, like music, painting, writing : their stream of phantasms is incredible.

The diversity of female experience and the variety of subjective categories that it explores, gives women's literature its unique quality. The female experience differs from person to person and from one country to the other. The Franco-American theories of Women's Discourse and patriarchal stricture cannot be applied to women's issues in the Afro-Asian framework. The impact of colonization and neo-colonization on the subaltern social structure and the womenfolk have not been explored fully as yet. Western notions of the female colonial being doubly subjected (1) by her colonizing masters, and (2) the patriarchal domination of her native social structures are highlighted and almost deified. Any step, legal or otherwise to alter this seemingly depressed position for women was hailed by the urbanized Westernized colonial as chivalric and accepted as a major justification of colonial rule. For instance, the abolition of 'sati' in 1829 was presented not merely as a case of 'White men... saving brown women from brown men' but as 'an actual narrative scenario of a single white man saving a brown woman from a mob of brown men.' The tendency to apply colonial precepts to native social structures and offer seemingly humanistic alternative to the in-built schemata, cannot be lauded if reviewed upon from a womanist angle.

To return to Kamala Das, her story is set in the once-matrilineal framework of the Nair Tharavad. Colonization and the imposition of Western notions of morality upon the native systems brought into currency her peculiar individual position. From the secure warmth of the Nalukettu, both Kamala and her mother are taken away into the rashness of a city culture that they are not accustomed to cope with. From a matrilineal and matrilocal framework that offered complete security to the women and their children were thrust into a Westernized patriarchal society, not quite equipped to deal with their new social responsibilities. The inadequacy of the Nair menfolk to cope with the emotional requirements of a family uprooted from its traditional backdrop is brought out by Kamala

Das's story. The women who were accustomed to gentle maternal care and consideration are at a loss in a male centered society.

Thus, we see how subaltern structures, supportive of the women's role in society, are broken down by patriarchal values drawn from the colonial masters. The woman (the matriarch) who had once controlled the whole family in the subaltern social is now reduced to a subjective degraded point. Talking about her mother's timidity which created an 'illusion of domestic harmony,' Kamala Das narrates :

> She was mortally afraid of the dark stranger who had come forward to take her out of the village and its security. She was afraid of her father and afraid of her uncle, the two men who plotted and conspired to bring for the first time into the family a bridegroom who neither belonged to any royal family nor was a Brahmin.

Such patriarchal authority would have been impossible in the unbroken Nair Tharavad where the woman was economically independent thereby had a voice of her own. It was only when the matriarchal structure was broken down by the phallocentric norms of a colonial culture that the woman's position was reduced to that of her female counterparts in the West.

In conclusion, I wish to draw attention to the idea of a common woman's identity as revealed through autobiography. Without by-passing or reducing belittling individual experiences, women's autobiography could help map out a new world of female space. In the post-colonial world any such effort should also take into consideration the subaltern structures of family hierarchy where the woman often occupied a position of prime importance. The role of women's autobiography in restructuring accepted norms of patriarchal discourse would thus be beyond question.

REFERENCES

1. Simone de Beauvoir. *The Second Sex*, 1949 rpt. (London : Picador, 1988): 174.
2. Gail Chester and Sigrid Nielson. *In Other Worlds : Writing as a Feminist.* London : Hutchinson, 1989.

3. Rosalind Brackenbury. "Women and Fiction: How We Present Ourselves and Others, *In Other Words*, 56.
4. Linda Anderson. "At the Threshold of the Self : Women and Autobiography," *Women's Writing : A Challenge to Theory*, ed. Moira Monteith (Sussex : The Harvester Press, 1986) : 59.
5. Kamala Das. *My Story*.
6. James Olney. "Some Versions of Memory/Some Versions of The Ontology of Autobiography," *Autobiography : Essays Theoretical and Critical*, ed. J. Olney (Princeton : Princeton UP, 1980) : 241.
7. Gail Chester and Sigrid Nielson. *In Other Words*, 17.
8. Irigaray. *The Sex which is not one*, tr. Catherine Porter, Ithaca: Cornell UP, (1985) : 218.
9. Elaine Showalter. "Towards a Feminist Poetics," *New Feminist Criticism*. (New York : Pantheon Books, 1985) : 131.
10. Hiline Cixons. "The Laugh of the Medusa," *Contemporary Literary Theory*, ed. Atkins (1989) : 80.
11. Rajeswari Sundara Rajan. *Real and Imagined Women : Gender Culture and Post-colonialism* (Routledge, 1993) : 42.

2

The Poems of Kamala Das : An Assessment

N.V. RAVEENDRAN*

Kamala Das has won renown as an Indian Poet writing in English overcoming the handicap of using an alien medium. As a poet of moods, rather than of methods, she has reiterated her attachment with the language she chose to write poetry. But her affinity for this medium is neither artificial nor superficial. In "An Introduction" (*Summer in Calcutta*), in a characteristically 'aggressive style' Kamala Das declares her preference for English as the medium of poetic communication :

> ...I am Indian, very brown born in
> Malabar, I speak three languages, write in
> Two, dream in one. Don't write in English, they said,
> English is not your mother tongue. Why not leave
> Me alone, critics, friends, visiting cousins,
> Everyone of you? Why not let me speak in
> Any language I like? The language I speak
> Becomes mine, its distortions, its queernesses
> All mine, mine alone.

There is implicit in this declaration whether or not English is a suitable medium for creative writing by Indians. The question 'why write in English?' has been in vogue. As far back as in 1945 the use of English Language as medium of literary expression was questioned.[1] N.K. Sidhanta was one of the first Indians to defend the use of English for artistic purposes. Sidhanta believed that the

*Lecturer, SVR NSS College, Vazhoor, Kerala.

artist has the right to use a medium of his choice. The summary of the prevailing views against the use of English as a creative medium is found in Jyotirmoy Datta :

> ...The Indo-English poet, even if he speaks English as it is spoken by those whose language it is, is locked up within himself, and though the inner music may sound enchanting to him, what a struggle must be put up to shut off those barbaric sounds ceaselessly bombard his eardrums! ...it deprives his imagination of the stimulus of living speech...the music of his verse too obvious, the lilt brazen, because his ears have been trained to listen only to the printed page, or, at best, to gramophone records of other poems.... What a nightmare of sterility have our writers in English created for us.[2]

The critics who oppose the use of English by Indian writers believe that mother-tongue interference will jar the writer's linguistic representation of his imagination and the product would be an intellectual jumble. Their opposition is enforced by Yeats's remark that no man can write or think with music except in his mother tongue.[3] But foster mothers, though rarely, give the effect of real mothers and the same may work in the case of language also. Poems in English by Indians, therefore, need not be mere sound and fury signifying nothing. The world-wide reputation some African and West Indian writers command may make it certain that real genii are not bound by linguistic restrictions. And now in India also seekers of fortune and fame are using this language to their best advantage (though at the expense of national/regional literature).

This does not imply that the Indo-English poet is always an expert in handling the English language. In fact a purposeful distortion of syntax is sometimes attempted to (artificially) effect 'defamiliarization.' But the successful 'new poets' of Indo-English tradition have always maintained a dignity of their own. Many of them, including Kamala Das, are bilinguals writing in their own mother-tongue. They are writers on their own right in that they have something genuine to say, and know how to say it in the language of their choice. Eventhough Kamala Das has written only a few poems in Malayalam, *e.g.* "Amma allathayitheernaval" ("The woman who ceased to be a mother"), "Yuva thalamura" ("Young generation"), "Cila vayanakkarodu randu vakku" ("A few words to the readers"), "Aparicita" ("The Stranger") in her mother tongue, she has proved that her attachment with poetry is profound.[4] This is because she is able to handle both English and her mother tongue well — she is able to select and arrange the linguistic elements that evoke the right kind of emotion.

This follows that the readers' approach to the English poetry produced in India should be purely aesthetic. Amalendu Bose makes this point clear :

> ...as readers of poetry we have to steer clear of non-aesthetic issues, content with considering poetry as poetry irrespective of the inherited or acquired character of the language used....[5]

Whether it be the tension between "two cultural and literary traditions"[6] or whether it be the product of the writer's urge to spread his fame overseas, poetry in English by Indians is a reality. In this paper the approach to this reality is aesthetic; the purpose is to examine how using an alien medium Kamala Das represents reality. However an assessment of the poetry of Kamala Das necessitates a review of the development of Indian Poetry in English from its very inception in the first decade of the nineteenth century.

The tradition of Indian poetry in English begins with Henry Louis Derozio (1831-1909). He was a poet as well as teacher of poetry who wrote on the lines of the English Romantics. Derozio wrote poetry on Nature and on social reformation, creating an impression among the young enthusiasts of that time. Next to Derozio in poetic creativity and influence was Kashiprosad Ghose (1809-1873). He was one of the first Indians to publish a volume of verse[7]. His poetry was 'derivative' and 'imitative.' Michael Madhusudan Dutt was a more enlightened poet who wrote in both Bengali and English. Like Derozio he too was influenced by the English Romantics.

These poets were interested more in the socio-cultural aspects than in the subtler realms of poetry. Directly or indirectly they participated in the Indian Renaissance movement in the nineteenth century. Toru Dutt (1856-1877), however, was an exception. She was the first Indian woman poet of renown writing in English on Indian legends, on love of nature and tender memories of childhood.

Rabindranath Tagore (1861-1941) entered the scene of the Indo-Anglian (Indo-English, we will be using these terms alternatively without any critical bearing) after making substantial contributions to Bengali literature. He wrote about "romantic longings, devotion to God and simple love of created things."[8] Tagore's mastery of the literary variety of the language was a great achievement : his was an example of how intricacies of language can create excellent poetry.

Sri Aurobindo Ghose (1872-1950) was more Indo-Anglian than Tagore in that his first literary medium was English rather than Bengali. He began his literary career as a writer devoted to the national movement and passing through different phases, ended up with a native fluency. However, Aurobindo's poetry cannot be separated from his philosophy, and for this very reason his status as an Indian writing poetry in English is difficult to assess.

The next among the series is Sarojini Naidu (1879-1949) who was a poet of passion and emotion — she wrote on Indian themes, on love and sorrow. Naidu is acclaimed as a genuine poet who wrote in a literary variety of English which she learned from the Cambridge literary circle.

After independence the Indian poetry in English shifted from the Romantic, socio-cultural and spiritual-transcendental school to a new kind based on personal experience. P. Lal and K. Raghavendra Rao called this new poetry as the espouser of "the private voice, especially because we live in an age that tends so easily to demonstrations of mass approval and hysteria."[9] It was for this reason that they decided to "celebrate the lyric from as the best suited for the capsule minded people."[10]

P. Lal, Nissim Ezekiel, A.K. Ramanujan, Shiv K. Kumar, Pritish Nandi and Kamala Das from a group that caused the new whirring in Indian poetry in English. They were followed by another generation of poets like Mamta Kalia, Gouri Deshpande, Eunice de Souza and Jayanta Mahapatra, all of whom wanting to explore the 'personal' and only very few achieving the objective. From among these poets Gouri Deshpande and Nissim Ezekiel are selected for examination in order to provide the reader a proper perspective.

Gauri Deshpande in her two books *Between Births*[11] and *Lost Love*[12] writes about love and relationship, a feature she shares with the rest of the Indo-English women poets. In accordance with the general trend her poems freely express her thoughts and feelings.

Gauri Deshpande's *Between Births* deals with the modern woman's rebellion against the rule of the male dictators. Poems in this collection figuratively project death as her lover and husband. In "Death," one of the poems in this collection, the female persona is shown as waiting for her "tardy lover" who is the husband/death. The "remorselessness" in the acceptance of a husband finds expression in "The Habit." The all-pervading power of marriage in the society makes the persona succumb to the husband/death. While the feminist harangue of this sort repeatedly occur in many for her poems, the confessionalists' confessions blossom in poems like "The Guest." Thus while marriage means death coitus means an act resulting in a feeling of emptiness :

You are gone now
The perfect mouth that kissed my words no longer by,
And as clouds heap and heap upon the west
I lie empty, barren and bereft....

("The Guest")

The apparent superficiality and lack of poeticality in the above lines is compensated for in the expression of tension and relaxation of the sexual kind using understatement :

Yet nothing happened
And I dreamt in the night of long travels
When I woke up the sky was heavy
And then it rained.

("A Change of Seasons")

"In Absentia," a poem in the collection *Lost Love* deals with love and the tension of parting. Here the lover is not the 'death bringer' but the carrier of pleasure : his absence means the absence of coitus which results in unhappiness. Thus :

Teeth clenched
Breath held
I wait for your coming
For, from that moment
I must start to live
The coming of your departure.

The personal feelings are skilfully represented in the "The Bridge," where the evocative qualities work in unison with the theme :

when its delicately balanced beauty
of pylon and span
That had linked and leapt
will disintegrate under your eye.

To sum up, Gauri Deshpande belongs to the feminist/ 'confessionalist' mode of Indian poetry in English. If the "love" poems relate her to the erotic poets of our tradition, the "death" poems speak for the feminist in her. The aptness of her imagery and diction has been applauded by Monika Varma[13] and her lack of proper literary competence has been brought to light by Eunice de Souza.[14]

Quest for identity, the dominant mood in confessional poetry, finds an important place in the poetry of Nissim Ezekiel. The man-woman relationship which paves way to the identification of the searcher's individuality is of great interest to him. In almost all of his poems Ezekiel explores the man-woman relation, that is, the role of women in relationship to men; this is where his poetic concepts contrast with those of the women poets like Gauri Deshpande and Kamala Das. Thus women in his poems are given the roles of mother, wife, sex object, whore and seductress — the roles human history has attributed to women.

In *A Time to Change*[15] Ezekiel portrays woman as seductress ("Something to Pursue"), a murderess ("The Old Woman") and a wife ("To a Certain Lady"). The union of man and woman in marriage is viewed as thesis-antithesis formula yielding synthesis which is frustration. The relationship begins this way ("To a Certain Lady") :

Life can be kept alive
By contact with the unknown and strange,
A feeling for the mystery
Of man and woman joined, exhaustion
At the act, desire for it again,...

And it gradually develops into :

There is no need to sulk,.... I shout at you
Because I love you, don't you know?
Well now, let's change the subject,
I can't make poetry out of this.

The theme of love and sex is repeated in *The Third.*[16] Despair as the end product of man's affairs with women is intimated in "Situation." Love ending in repulsion is presented thus :

They left reluctantly but took with them despair.
A dozen heads were turned on them with prying eyes.
He shook her hands, but wished to stroke her waiting hair
And dragged his feet in going home to tell his lies.

"The Couple" in *Hymns in Darkness*[17] is another poem treating the superficiality of man-woman relation. The woman in this poem is a whore and seductress :

In that moment of mutual deception,
She was truly quite beautiful
and almost lovable
She did it prettily enough,
demonstrating
With child like glee
a trick or two.

Ezekiel's *The Exact Name*[18] contains the poem "Night of the Scorpion" which vividly captures the ways and beliefs of Indian villagers. The woman in this poem is the symbol of tolerance and protection. The lines run on :

I watched the holyman perform his rites
to tame the poison with an incantation,
After twenty hours,
it lost its sting
My mother only said

Thank God the scorpion pricked on me
and spared my children.

In short Nissim Ezekiel's poetry explores the self — poetry to him is the expression of personality, not getting away from it. While finding expression to his inner moods he describes the people he encounters, especially the women.

The foregoing has been an attempt to outline the tradition of Indian writing in English, the background against which the poetry of Kamala Das is projected. Being a multilingual nation inhabiting people with diverse views to life and literature, the poetry by Indians, whether in English or in any of the Indian languages, will show subtle shades of difference. Gauri Deshpande's world view might differ from Kamala Das's and Nissim Ezekiel's from both. While change is effected by time, space and culture, it is interesting to note that each of them bear the signet of a common tradition. In the following pages an attempt will be made to outline what makes the poetry of Kamala Das a unique phenomenon and at the same time gives it the flavour of a composite poetic tradition.

Kamala Das's first collection of poems *Summer in Calcutta* appeared when Indo-Anglian poets had shifted from the themes belonging to the colonial past to personal themes. The confessional mode was already established in the English speaking countries, especially in America. The Indian women poets with their love for the intensely personal confessional mode and with certain amount of attraction for the feminist views were all actively writing poetry. While their attempt was to explore the 'self' in depth, most of them could only scratch the surface. However the poetry of Kamala Das has been hailed as excellent because of the apparent imaginative daring, stylistic innovation, richness of energy, and music. All these qualities spring from her poetic genius; she is a natural poet, not a semi-skilled craftsman trying to construct poetic artefacts. Kamala Das is an investigator of the impulses, one who is obsessed with the flow of inner experience. Being a natural poet her poems may show different levels of poeticality, depending upon the nature of the spatio-temporal effect on her senses and intellect. The natural poet, promoted by the spatio-temporal effect, goes on writing till the inspiration fades away. The following words of the Soviet poet

Bella Akhmadulina throw light upon the way the natural poet would generate poetry :

> After I have lived in some faraway place for about ten days, I suddenly hear a sound...the necessary word is found. And then I write and write and for twenty four hours a day without a break until the guiding sound has faded away.[19]

An almost similar idea is contained in Kamala Das's words :

"I write only at night when I am left alone and every one else is asleep. Then the world suddenly comes to focus, becomes more my own."[20] These opinions by the poets have to do with the way their poems are to be approached. The sudden excitement of the poet's creative faculty by some impulse generated by stimulus in a spatio-temporal context results in poetry.

Kamala Das's poery is spontaneous, straightforward and simple. She opens up for the reader new fields of feelings and emotions in an earnest manner. What she presents before the reader is a synthesis of rare and contrasting thoughts of lonely minds. She perceives the world as one perceives it in a dream. Though she believes that she has not achieved the emotional maturity to write sublime poetry,[21] her heart flows in words abounding in sensual rhythms and soulful laments. The experience she concretises is her's as well as anybody else's. Kamala Das has glorified love in her poems. Love to her is a kind of beautiful religion of which sex is a part. As she maintains, her love is not mere lust; but as she likes it to be demonstrative her preference is for the sexual kind.[22]

On another plane we find in her poetry an alert and inquisitive approach to life. She draws inspiration from the simple, the sad and the gorgeous events in everyday life. The evenings in the old Nalapat house, the silence around the hanging corpse of a maid servant, the frenzied dance of the eunuchs in the burning Calcutta afternoon, the smell of death in the hospital wards, the Anamalai hills, a brown comrade in a Sri Lankan street, a vigorous but loveless lover, all inspire her to write. And she writes, dipping the sharp end of her imagination in her simple but sensitive, sensual but sad heart, about the mundane and ethereal and the reader witnesses the coalescence of various emotions in all her four published books of verse.

With her personal experience at the core Kamala Das has succeeded in writing delightful poetry and has gained and applause of the people who once showered on her the venom of negative criticism. It is with extreme sincerity that she pictures her quest for identity. It appears in the song of a heart that longs for sexual satisfaction, in the recollection of the purity and playfulness of the childhood, in the broken womanhood, in the love of the grandmother, in the cruelty and hypocrisy of men, in the painful realization of failing youth and approaching old age and in the despair of old age itself.

The poems in *Summer in Calcutta* (1965), *The Descendants* (1967), *Old Playhouse and Other Poems* (1973), *Collected Poems* Vol. 1, (1984), and "Anamala poems" (in *Indian Literature*, 28,2) deal mainly with her own personal experience in relation to time and space. Two poems in *Summer in Calcutta*, eight in *Collected Poems* Vol. 1, and four out of the seven poems (one repetition) published in *Indian Literary Review* 7,2 express concern over the prevailing atmosphere at home and abroad. With the exception of such poems the majority of her poems present her personal ecstasies, sorrows and convictions in a way that could shatter the ideas that an average Indian had on his surroundings at the time of their composition. (Thanks to globalization! we are learning to shatter everything ours). Devendra Kohli who finds a "passionate sincerity" in her poetry says that "she can hypnotise one with the weight of her personal passion which colours her attitude to the external world....[23] This observation hints at the aesthetics of Kamala Das which has its roots in her own energy and desire. This is apparent in a good number of her poems.

Among the love poems in *Summer in Calcutta* (hereafter SC) "Love" is typical in that it expresses the female persona's contentment in having found a lover :

> Now that I Love You
> Curled like an old mongrel
> My life lies, content,
> In you....

Passing from the expression of contentment in love to the physical aspects, she speaks about her love for the male body in "The Looking Glass" (*The Descendants* hereafter DS). It is nearly an erotic poem as it describes the male and female bodies giving exciting details :

Notice the perfection
Of his limbs, his eyes reddening under
Shower, the shy walk across the bathroom floor,
Dropping towels, and the jerky way he
Urinates. And all the fond details that make
Him male and your only man. Gift him all,
Gift him what makes you woman, the scent of
Long hair, the musk of sweat between the breasts,
The warm shock of menstrual blood, and all your
Endless female hungers.

The physical details and the explicit expression of lust are given additional dimensions in "In Love" (SC) :

...his mouth like pale and
Carnivorous plants reaching
Out for me and the sad lie
Of my unending lust.

Linda Hess says that the poem is a superb example of poetic talent making it one of the excellent pieces in the *Summer in Calcutta Collection*.[24] The consummation of this sort of expression of sexuality is there in "A child in the Factory" (SC). A vivid description of coitus marks such a climax — climax in form and content :

One by one, the intelligences fall, the
pumps the pipes, throbbing
Mechanisms, and with a final
Angry glow, the factory
Dies.

H.M. Williams maintains that the eroticism in her poetry "hover on the edge of a kind of concupiscent neuroticism which we find in a different way in the best seventeenth century English poems of the so called 'metaphysical' mode."[25] However Kamala Das does not share the wit and wisdom of the 'metaphysicals' for whom eroticism was but a way of exhibiting their own peculiar approach to poetry and life.

The frustration in married life and the breaking of the emotional ties between husband and wife are symbolically presented in "The Bangles" (SC). The bangles, in some parts of India, are considered a symbol of matrimonial relation. Kamala Das seems to present the discontentment and disharmony in married relationship restricted to bed-rooms in the following lines :

...At night,
In sleep, the woman lashes
At pillows with bangled arms; in
Vain she begs bad dreams to fade.
The man switches on the light and
Looks into her face with his
grey, pitiless eyes...

The woman sufferer in this way realizes the fallacy in married relations. In such poems Kamala Das portrays the tribulations of the woman who has lost anchorage in the turbulent sea of human life. The persona is denied of love and comfort. The husband all the times remains complacent, making her act according to his whims. The disgust and anger in the woman's heart is expressed in a typically feminine way in "The Stone Age" (*Old Playhouse and Other Poems*, hereafter OP) :

Fond husband, ancient settler in the mind
Old fat spider, weaving webs of bewilderment,
Be kind. You turn me into a bird of stone, a granite
Dove, you build around me a shabby drawing room,
And stroke my pitted face absent mindedly while
You read.

The revelation that love and matrimony are poles apart prompts Kamala Das's persona to search for a lover. Though the love affair gives her excitement in the beginning it is accompanied by disillusionment. Her lover is incapable of giving her a blissful experience. A deep sense of frustration is thus expressed in "The Freaks" (SC) in the form of a question thrown into the air :

Can this man with
nimble finger tips unleash

Nothing more alive than the
Skins lazy hungers?

The realization of the futility of the endeavour and the awareness that the 'other' cannot satisfy her is implied in the rhetorical question : "Who can/Help us who have lived so long/And have failed in love?" Cohabitation does not give her real pleasure. It results in the feeling of emptiness and stillness. The boredom of a pleasureless sexual encounter makes her heart "an empty cistern" which fills itself "With coiling snakes of silence." Arlene R.K. Zide holds that Kamala Das's themes transcend the 'personal' because what she attempts to poetise is the "universal experience of women."[26] Zide argues that the self explorations of Kamala Das are beyond the feminist haranguing because they have a universal appeal.

The detachment from the world of reality and the venturing in the world of imagination, the eternal longing for true love, is the theme of "Ghanashyam" (*Collected Poems,* Vol. I hereafter CP I). The persona longs for Krishna, the 'eternal lover,' like the mythical 'chataka' bird that waits for ever for the celestial water to quench its thirst.

Ghanashyam,
You have like a koel built your nest in the arbour of my heart.
My life until now a sleeping jungle is at last astir with music
You lead me along a route that I have never known before
But at each turn when I near you
Like a spectral flame you vanish.

The portrayal of marriage and the husband in her poems in relation to the self and the yearning for fulfilment projected in the dream of union with an elusive lover are based on sex. The antithetical attitudes of men and women play an important role in the construction of Kamala Das's imagery. That her poetic imagination, to a considerable extent, is based on sexuality, is implicitly marked in her poem "An introduction" (SC) :

...I met a man, loved him. Call
Him not by any name, he is every man

Who wants a woman, just as I am every
Woman who seeks love.

The tension between desire and disillusionment is the sign of poetic strength in a good number of poems in Kamala Das's four volumes of poetry. The projection of self is most often constrained by her own desire for sex and the longing for release from the male body. Thus Kamala Das's persona alternates between the 'libertine' and liberated.

The self image that Kamala Das projects in her poems is one tormented by unfulfilled desire. This desire for sex and the search for fulfilment is the fulcrum of her aesthetics of sensuality. She finds the men emotionally deficient and incapable of possessing a passionate regard for concrete reality. Kamala Das's view of the world of reality is blurred by her view that positive male figures are absent in the world. As a result the seeming male indifference in attributing to women a capacity for individuation is condemned in her poems of self exploration. The sex based aspects of her observations about men are more complex than the same in her contemporaries like Gauri Deshpande. However she shares with men an erotic consciousness of the everyday world which is depicted in the sensual imagery of her poems. The way she handles the sex theme finally relates the self image she builds up to sex as such in all its vigour.

Unfulfilled desire is the theme of "The Dance of the Eunuchs" (SC). The poem has a faint similarity with the grotesque dance of the mendicants in Wole Soyinka's play *Madmen and Specialists*.[27] The theme however is different — the eunuchs stand for infertility and unfulfilled desire. They represent the "vacant ecstasy" of the narrator. The "hot sun," the "fiery gulmohur," "harsh voices," "Melancholy songs," beating of the drums, and the funeral pyre constitute a combination of visual and auditory images suggesting "vacant ecstasy." Anisur Rahman claims that the images in Kamala Das's poems undergo metamorphosis and become symbols giving strength and vigour to her poetry.[28] His discussion on the use of words in her poetry shows that she is well at home with the English language — her repertoire of English vocabulary is sufficient to formally represent her vision as a poet.

Nostalgia dominates the poem "A Hot Noon in Malabar" (SC), where the persona dreams about her home in Malabar during a hot afternoon. The sun at its zenith gives the effect of a burning furnace and the body is equally hot, burning with lust. The "brick-ledged well" offers a contrast, the cool and refreshing depth. A sort of double meaning exists in almost all of the lines : while being in a nostalgic mood the speaker is not without sensual feelings.

Kamala Das's treatment of the personal theme has already received attention. In "The Flag" (SC) she unveils the futility of national pride when poverty and blood-shed sow misery among the multitude. She laments :

Foor flag, dear one,
Your pride is lost, it is time to leave the sky
And fall and hide
Your shame beneath this blood drenched Indian soil
And lie there and rot...

This expresses her deep concern for the people outside the personal circle. In "The Return of Hitler,"[29] she is found to be identifying herself with the suffering of Sri Lankan Tamils.

Hitler rose from the dead; he demanded
Yet another round of applause; he hailed
The robust Aryan blood, the sinister
Brew that absolves a man of his sins and
Gives him right to kill his former friends.
The Dark Dravidian laid his three-year old child
On his lap, little mother, he said, close your eyes
and sleep....

Elena J. Kalinikova, an East European commentator, while calling Kamala Das a love poet modifies and extends the existing opinions about her vision to the broader regions of humanism where life is viewed not as mere birth, copulation and death.

> In a general chorus of voices asserting the fear before death in one way or another, absurdity of human aspirations and emptiness of feelings, is sharply singled out. Optimism fills both the types of poems : poems in which she narrates with bitterness the misfortunes of her compatriots and the poems

> which are fraught with philosophical meditations about happiness and sufferings, about life and death. But assertion of life is especially perceptible in her lyrical cycles about love, particularly in her collection, *The Descendants*.[30]

Calling Kamala Das a purely confessional poet means not doing justice to her vision as a poet. As we have seen in the preceding observation, Kamala Das has the capacity to transcend the purely personal and embrace the non-personal and finally merge with it. While her quest for identity makes her a confessional poet, many of her poems express deep sympathy for the sufferers — be it about an old woman's 'longing lingering look' from behind the window bars, or be it about a bleeding brown comrade in Sri Lanka, her poems initiate the fusion of her self with the surrounding.

It would be interesting to look at the poems of Kamala Das with a view to finding out certain similarities and contrasts. Nissim Ezekiel's artistic talents offer a better field for comparison and contrast with Kamala Das's. Ezekiel's views while being that of a confessionalist, differs from Kamala Das's in his traditional approach to the roles of women. We have seen that women in most of his poems live in a male dominated society. While sex and disillusionment form part of the poetry of both, Kamala Das celebrates a free woman-hood — she gives a free individuality to her woman persona. To this effect Subhas Chandra Saha makes the following observation : "Ezekiel's quality of restraint, dignity and artistic sobriety is set off by Mrs. Das's intense flow of emotion reaching the stream of consciousness level of expression. Mrs. Das has a force of passion that impels her to talk as her heart likes."[31] H.M. Williams in his survey of Indo-Anglian literature, finds similarity between Nissim Ezekiel and Kamala Das in that they are both honest in presenting details. He thinks that the most attractive elements in Ezekiel's poetry — the honest saga of self discovery — is there in Kamala Das's poems also. Williams finds a companion for Kamala Das in Shiv K. Kumar in the treatment of love : both of them exhibit certain amount of bitterness and pessimism.[32] Ramanujan, another contemporary of Kamala Das, treats the "self" theme in a slightly different manner. While Kamala Das's is an incessant quest for 'self,' laden with sensuality and compassion for fellow beings, Ramanujan identifies himself with history. M. Sivaramakrishna's observation seems to point to this aspect :

> If the implicit mode in Ramanujan arises from a felt tension between self and history the differentia of Kamala Das's poetry is a negation of history and total preoccupation with self — a preoccupation which accounts for both individual talent before her poetry and the absence of a corrective tradition which can prevent self preoccupation from being an obsession.[33]

"Total preoccupation with self" is not a wholly agreeable point — a good number of her poems treat non-personal themes. Out of the three poets, only Ezekiel seems to follow metrics. Ramanujan's style is elliptical and colloquial, and Kamala Das, while maintaining harmony of sounds in some poems, mostly flows out passion packed words.

A comparison of Kamala Das with Gauri Deshpande would bring out certain qualities of the former. A.K. Srivastava and Smitha Sinha who have attempted such a comparison has this to say :

> Each of them works out an idiom for the expression of a uniquely feminine sensibility! Kamala Das goes about in her disarmingly uninhibited confessionals which despite their shocking gestures have in them a deeply religious flavour ("A man is a season"), and Gauri Deshpande acquires the same stance by exploiting areas of feelings although her poetry has certain cloying effect and lacks Kamala Das's aplomb and genius for the right word ("The Female of the species").[34]

A passing reference to Sarojini Naidu who is noted for her lyrical ability would make the foregoing further clear. While Naidu never exposes her personal experiences Kamala Das is a thorough investigator of the intensely personal experience. Under the influence of the English Romantics Naidu traces her identity in Nature, writing about its 'beauteous forms,' while Kamala Das attempts to explore the stark realities within and around her. However, they seem to share one thing, irrespective of the gap in time, namely sensibility. But unlike Sarojini Naidu Kamala Das builds a dramatic framework to transfer her experiences to the reader. Stressing on the originality of the modern Indo-English love poets Subas C. Saha observes :

> Sarojini Naidu is a notable example of ordinariness and absence of originality, she writes a love poem "If You Call Me" a few lines of which show her command over the flow of English language, but also the deplorable lack of ingenuity and originality (which is betrayed by imitative fluid style and repetition of words and images in the manner of Shelley and Tennyson).[35]

It is worth mentioning here what C.N. Srinath says about Kamala Das :

> There is conspicuous craftsmanship, introspection and self analysis in her poetry that has given it character. It is the sensitive awareness of her surroundings, its sordidness, its boredom, ugliness and horror that is the strength of her poetry.[36]

It seems to be appropriate to end this discussion with a brief note on Kamala Das's versification. While traditional prosody is gradually losing its hold among the poets in the English speaking countries, it is rarely seen employed in Indo-English poetry. R. Parthasarathy observes in this connection : "In our time poetry is becoming increasingly concise. It is moving towards metaphor."[37] The reason for this preference for verse is implicit in the following :

> Apart from Ezekiel, the poets have little or no use for traditional prosody. This isn't as surprising as it may appear. Prosody is essentially aural, and requires a keen ear and not all poets possess it. The emphasis is therefore, almost entirely on the visual as opposed to the aural elements in verse.[38]

Kamala Das's preference for free verse may be due to her lack of competence in metrics. However free verse employs occasionally conventional devices such as assonance, alliteration and rhyme. What is flouted is the count of stresses and the rate of occurrence of syllables within the line. In free verse the rhythm deciding factor seems to be phrasal syntax; modern poets have done away with the frequent use of pauses. Hence according to the traditional view the free verse is irregular in structure. This, however, is compensated for by the change in the approach to the language of poetry in general. Idioms and phrases belonging to prose, sound symbolism and even illogical sequences are used as for grounding devices. A stylistic approach thus assumes importance in the interpretation of the poetry of a writer like Kamala Das. This, however, is out of our concern as the purpose has been restricted to an assessment of Mrs. Das's poetry with reference to the works of her contemporaries like Nissim Ezekiel and Gauri Deshpande.

NOTES

1. See the discussion on the use of English as creative medium in N.K. Sidhanta, "English," *The Indian Literatures of Today : A Symposium*, ed. B. Kumarappa (Bombay : The International Book House, 1947) : 24-48.
2. Jyotirmoy Datta, "On Caged Chaffinches and Polyglot Parrots," *Quest*, 28, Jan-Mar 1961 : 28-29.
3. W.B. Yeats, *The Letters of W.B. Yeats*, ed. Allan Wade (New York : Macmillan, 1955) : 834.
4. See Kamala Das, *Bhayan ente nisavastram* (Calicut : Mathrubhoomi Printing and Publishing House, 1986).
5. Amalendu Bose, "Modern Indian Poetry in English," *Indian Literature*, 13,1 (1970) : 55.
6. Homi Bhabha, "Indo-Anglian Attitudes," *TLS,* 21 Apr. 1975 : 445.
7. For a consideration see Iyengar, 37.
8. H.M. Williams, 29.
9. P. Lal and K. Raghavendra, introduction, *Modern Indo-Anglian Poetry* quoted by H.M. Williams, 109-110.
10. Lal and Raghavendra, quoted by H.M. Williams, 109-110.
11. Gauri Deshpande, *Between Births* (Calcutta : Writers Workshop, 1968).
12. Gauri Deshpande, *Lost Love* (Calcutta : Writers Workshop, 1970).
13. Monika Varma, *Facing Four* (Calcutta : Writers Workshop, 1973) : 13-24.
14. Eunice de Souza, "Kamala Das, Gauri Deshpande, Mamta Kalia," *Quest*, Jan-Feb. (1972) : 86-87.
15. Nissim Ezekiel, *A Time to Change* (London : Fortune Press, 1952).
16. Nissim Ezekiel, *The Third* (Bombay : The Strand Bookshop, 1959).
17. Nissim Ezekiel, *Hymns in Darkness* (Delhi : Oxford UP, 1976).

18. Nissim Ezekiel, *The Exact Name* (Calcutta : Writers Workshop, 1965).
19. Bella Akhmadulina, Interview, *Soviet Literature* 6, 483 (1988) : 140.
20. Atma Ram, *Interviews with Indian English Writers* (Calcutta : Writers Workshop, 1983) : 81.
21. See Kamala Das, Interview, *Katha* 86 (1984) : 12.
22. *Katha* 86 (1984) : 13.
23. Devendra Kohli, "Passionate Sincerity in Indian Poetry in English," *The Journal of Commonwealth Literature*, 9, 1 (1974) : 23.
24. Linda Hess, "Post-Independence Indian Poetry in English," *Considerations*, ed. Meenakshi Mukherjee (Bombay : Allied Publishers, 1977) : 40.
25. H.M. Williams, 117.
26. Arlene R.K. Zide, rev. of *The Old Playhouse and Other Poems*, by Kamala Das, *Journal of South Asian Literature* 16, 1 (1981) : 239.
27. Wole Soyinka, *Wole Soyinka : Collected Plays* 2 (Oxford : Oxford UP, 1974) : 215-276.
28. Anisur Rahman, *Expressive From in the Poetry of Kamala Das* (New Delhi : Abhinav Publications, 1981) : 37.
29. Kamala Das, "The Return of Hitler," *Indian Literary Review* 3,2 (1985) : 29.
30. Elena J. Kalinikova, *Indian English Literature : A Perspective* (Ghaziabad : Vimal Prakashan, 1974) : 202.
31. Subhas Chandra Saha, *Modern Indo-Anglian Love Poetry* (Calcutta : Writers Workshop, 1971) : 39.
32. H.M. Williams, 117.
33. M. Sivaramakrishna, "The Tongue in English Chains : Indo-English Poetry Today," *Indian Poetry in English : A Critical Assessment*, eds. Vasant A. Sahane and M. Sivaramakrishna (Madras : Macmillan, 1980) : 16-17.
34. A.K. Srivastava and Smitha Sinha, "New Voices : Animadversions on Recent Indo-Anglian Love Poetry," *Indian Writing in English*, ed. Krishna Nandan Sinha (New Delhi : Heritage Publishers, 1971) : 121.
35. Saha, 11.
36. C.N. Srinath, "Contemporary Indian Poetry in English," *Literary Criterion* 2,3 (1968) : 61.
37. R. Parthasarathy, *Ten Twentieth Century Indian Poets* (Delhi : Oxford UP, 1976) : 9.
38. Parthasarathy, 10.

3

A Feminist Voice — A Study of Kamala Das's Poems

RAMESH KUMAR GUPTA*

In the contemporary Indian literary scenario, Kamala Das occupies a prominent position as a poetess of talent and artistry. She, as a major Indian poetess in English, has attracted international attention by virtue of her bold, uninhibited articulation of feminine urges alongwith other women poets like Gauri Deshpande, Mamata Kalia, de Souza and others. Mrs. Das has written some books of poems *i.e.*, "Summer in Calcutta," "The Descendants," "The Old Playhouse" and other Poems. Her anguished affirmation of independence is available in her autobiography, "My Story." Das's quest for identity is directly the progeny of an old social set up, oriented towards the total annihilation of the feminine personality. Love and sex are, no doubt, the leitmotif of her poetry but the depth of her distress seems to have left a constant sting in her soul, and that does invest her identity with a certain tincture of pangs. As K.R.S. Iyengar points out the subject of her poetry : "Love is crucified in sex, and sex defiles itself again and again."[1] M.K. Naik depicts the same figure : "The most obvious (and to casual reader, colourful) feature of Kamala Das's poetry is the uninhibited frankness with which she talks about sex referring nonchalantly to 'the musk of sweat between the breasts,' 'the warm shock of menstrual blood;' and even 'my pubis.' "[2] I attempt to explain the feminist voice through some of her poems in which Mrs. Das has projected a new device to liberate the women from the bondage of slavery in man-dominated society.

*Research Scholar, Department of English, Jai Prakash University, Chapra, Bihar.

"Summer in Calcutta" depicts the sensuous absorption of sunlight which may be thought a metaphor for poetess's destination. The male-chauvinism on the feminine psyche is reduced when she lets herself participate in the world of nature and stimulation of life independently. At the conclusion of the poem Mrs. Das affirms :

How
Brief the term of my
Deviation, how brief
Your reign when I with
Glass in hand, drink, drink
And drink again this
Juice, of April Suns.

The poem records the subjugation of male's hegemony over females. The poetess refers to the sensuous absorption of sunlight which is known as a metaphor for her fascination with life :

"The April Sun, squeezed
Like an orange in
My glass? I sip the
Fire, I drink and drink
Again, I am drunk,
Yes, but on the gold
Of suns."

(*The Old Playhouse and Other Poems,* p. 24)

The poetess's response to life is not merely voluptuous but also emotional :

"Venom now flows through
My veins and fills my
Mind with unhurried
Laughter?

Mrs. Das thinks that the venom flowing through veins enters her psyche and fills with unhurried humour.

In the poem 'An Introduction,' Mrs. Das presents the naked truth and places words boldly in such a manner in which people have their no oncomings. Her expression becomes dramatic, strong and against old images :

"I was child and later they
Told me I grew, for became tall, my limbs

Swelled and one or two places sprouted hair. When
I asked for love, not knowing what else to ask
For, he drew a youth of sixteen into the
Bedroom and closed the door. He did not beat me
But my sad woman-body felt so beated.
The weight of my breasts and womb crushed me.
I shrank Pitifully."

(*The Old Playhouse and Other Poems*, pp. 26-27)

The tone of the poem appears hysterical, as Juliet Mitche says : "Hysteria is the woman's simultaneous acceptance and refus l of the organization of sexuality under patriarchal capitalism. It is simultaneously what woman can do both to be feminine and to refuse femininity. Within patriarchal discourse."[3]

In "The Looking Glass" Mrs. Das portrays the nudity of the stark reality of life through physical imagery being biasless :

"Stand nude before the glass with him
So that he sees himself the stronger one
And believes it so, and you so much more
Softer, younger, lovelier...
...and the jerky way he urinates."

But it is woman who offers to man the sensual pleasure of her body :

"Gift him what makes you woman, the scent of
Long hair, the musk of sweat between the breasts,
The warm shock of menstrual blood, and all your
Endless female hungers."

(*The Descendants*)

Mrs. Das presents a feminist movement through her poetry. She discovers the male-hegemony from the inner care of her feminine consciousness. Mrs. Das's personality has its irrelaxable anchors in sexual love and when it is refused she feels her life meaningless, barren and waste land, she bursts out in the poem "The Suicide" :

"O sea, I am fed up,
I want to be simple,
I want to be loved.

... ...

If love is not to be had,
I want to be dead."

In "Jaisurya" Mrs. Das's effect continues to search the reality through life, nature and herself. She evaluates the sex by her quest of the birth of new life :

"Out of the mire of a moonless night was
He born, Jaisurya, my son, as out of
The wrong is born the right and out of night
The sun-drenched golden day."

Mrs. Das's inquisition for reality ends pleasantly after the birth of Jaisurya. She has delineated her feminist voice through sex-imagery. Her search for identity is sex-oriented. In the context of feminist voice, Mr. Das has presented Indian English poetry a new discourse : the discourse of woman's corporal language from the point of view of woman. To communicate the vision of truth Mrs. Das uses words boldly, speaking in a manner in which people have not spoken before. The poem 'Summer in Calcutta' celebrates the poetess's mirthful share in life, but when read between the lines, the poem records the poetess's awareness about the male-chauvinism over woman. Mrs. Das has never found fulfilment in her emotional life. 'When one man went out, another came in.' "For years I have run from one gossamer to another, my own captive" (*Captive, The Descendants*).

"The Old Playhouse" portrays how incurably her fostered dreams and destinations have been oppressed in the company of her spider-like husband : "He no longer calls for me, he no longer comes to me, or stands at the open window to the smile at me." This theme finds repeated expression in her poems. In "The conflagration," she asks herself sarcastically : "Woman, is the happiness, this lying buried beneath a man?" Here Kamala Das has become the mouthpiece of all women, suffering passive pathos in a male hegemonic set up. Her personal life is responsible for her hastily diving into the uncharted sea of sexuality. Her husband's pride of his having had contacts with "Sluts and nymphomaniacs" creates a revolt in her heart against the very institution of arranged wedding. So, she ventures upon "a hectic love life with small capital...just a pair of beautiful breasts and a faint musk-rat smell in my perspiration." *De facto* she was tender and deeply emotional and desired for a better and more sympathetic and considerate conjugal life by an unfeeling husband who required her "break saccharine into your tea and to offer at the right moment and vitamins." Her sincerity and her deep humiliation can be easily appreciated by the woeful observation made by her : "Cowering beneath your monstrous ego, I ate the magic leaf and became a dwarf." This subjugation to "dwarfhood" should culminate into a hectic career if promiscuous love, which is puzzling. Her husband gave her freedom to enjoy sex according to her own choices also sounds bewildering, but such examples are found in society, especially in cities : Kamala Das herself says that adultery is common with women residing in cities. The feminine inquisition however rebels against the very basis of antique ethos, against all established order. The antithesis has initiated in Indian women's outlook in as much as it is felt that women cannot evolve their full individuality in family or society within the traditional bounds.

Love and sex are the leitmotif of her poetry but her profound frustration seems to have left a perpetual biting in her soul. The contrast between the happy security of childhood under the loving guidance of her grandmother and her quest for love as an adult is acutely brought out in the poem, "The Suicide" :

"I had a house in Malabar
and a pale-green pond.
I did all my growing there
in the bright summer months.
I swam about the floated
I lay speckled green and gold
In all the hours of the sun,
Until
My grandmother cried,
Darling, you must stop this bathing now,
You are much too big to play
Naked in the pond."

The memory of her childhood under the grandmother's loving roof provide a silver lining to her otherwise sex-clouded personality. Mrs. Das's several poems are about the warmth of her childhood and the family home in Kerala. But the loss of her grandmother's affection continues to torment her inner spirit :

"The only secrets I always
Withhold
are that I am so alone
and that I miss my grandmother."

(*Composition*)

Kamala Das present warmth of her childhood in her several poems. Like other South Indian poets, such as Ramanujan, Parthasarathy, Meena Agrawal and Sharat Chandra, Kamala writes of memories of childhood, family relations and family's house. Now she has no occasion to affirm her identity, that is, her distinctive selfhood, which possibly emerges in adverse situations.

Mrs. Das's marital life if based on incongruity. She was married at the early age of fifteen to a bank official, *tout a fait* insensitive to a young girl's longings. Kamala Das is bound to do the domestic duties in the family against her tender feelings and yearnings for emotional involvement. This sort of existence in her husband's home presents the miserably predicament of a woman — an instance of 'prey and predatory' image. The male domination on feminine psyche can be diminished and dilapidated by woman when she lets herself participate in the world of nature and in the amelioration of her status independently. Compelled by the circumstances Kamala Das presently deserts her Hindu religion and avows the religion of Islam putting on a veil. Her transformation of religion is a vivid picture of woman's identity and liberty. She is not a 'gentle-cow' of M.R. Anand's "The Old Woman and the Cow." She is literate so she knows how to combat against the age-old customs in the society. That is why she presents a new paradigm of the coming generation in India and abroad.

In the contemporary literature, written by women, the feminine voice revolves largely round claim for perfect freedom in personal matters, chiefly in relation to love and sex. The old customs yielding place to the all-pervading spirit of modernism which has crystallized predominantly in the elimination of the *status quo* in every conceivable walk of life. It appears perfectly natural that Indian women elevate their voice against the established order and try to affirm their distinct identity breaking the traditional taboos as to love and sex which is the outcome of male dominated society.

Thus, Kamala Das is a contemporary Indian poetess quite conscious of her artistic design and purpose as well as of her responsibility towards her vision. Here is undoubtedly a feminist voice articulating the hopes and oppressions, the concerns and tensions, of womankind. Explicitly, she writes about love, sex and marriage — all well within her experience and awareness. Her poetic voice imbued with a feminine-*cum*-feminist sensibility is typically her own and it cannot be confused with anyone else's.

NOTES

1. K.R.S. Iyengar. *Indian Writing in English* (New Delhi : Sterling Publishers, 1983) : 677.
2. M.K. Naik. *A History of Indian English Literature* (New Delhi : Sahitya Akademi, 1982) : 208.
3. Juliet Mitchel. "Feminism, Narrative and Psychoanalysis," reprinted in *Modern Criticism and Theory*, ed. David Lodge (London and New York : Longman, 1988) : 427.

4

Kamala Das : 'The Tragedy of Life is not Death but Growth'

O.J. THOMAS*

Kamala Das writes her autobiography into every one of her poem. Some doubt her sincerity, while others call her a hypocrite in a lamb's woolly skin, to present herself as honest, but none denies the freshness and novelty in her poems which like a stone fresh from a wild stream, go blindly to hit and wound our conscience, knowingly or unknowingly. Where did she acquire this personal idiom, which has set her apart from others? How did she get initiated into a search for one's own personality and its diverse faces? To understand this, one should go into her life and into her poems.

I

Kamala Das was born in Southern Malabar on the 31st of March, 1934. Her mother, Balamaniamma, is a renowned Malayalam poetess. She was married to K. Madhava Das at the tender age of fifteen. Her famous collections of poems include *Summer in Calcutta* (1965, Everest Press, Delhi.), *The Descendants* (1967, Writer's Workshop, Calcutta), *The Old Play House* (1973, Macmillan). Her autobiography *My Story,* attracted the attention of the world and got translated into no less than fourteen languages. She is a bilingual writer. Her Short Stories are very popular in Malayalam. She uses a pseudonym, Madhavikutty in her writings in Malayalam. She was

*Head, Department of English, J.N. Govt. College, Port Blair.

awarded The Kerala Sahitya Akademi prize in 1967 for her collection of stories entitled *Thanuppu,* meaning in English, "Cold." She won the Asian PEN Poetry prize in 1964, for her poem *"The Sirens."* She also won the Chimanlal Award for 'Fearless Journalism.' She functioned as the poetry Editor of *The Illustrated Weekly of India* for one year, from 1971-1972.

II

A Poetess of Love and Pain

The publication of *Summer in Calcutta* changed the history of Indo-Anglian poetry, especially of women writers. It was a time when "...Indian women had moved on from such colonial and nationalist themes as the rewriting of legends, praise of peasants and from general ethical statements to writing about personal experiences. While outmoded diction and sentiments were at last overtaken in favour of a more contemporary and less artificial manner, the subject matter of the women poets was often limited to well-meaning platitudes about romantic love, which were treated without depth, complexity, interest or even the projection of much emotion."[1]

Summer in Calcutta, presented to the Indian reader a different type of poetry. Earlier poets looked at the Holy Books, Historical characters for their themes, while she looked into her own self. Her poems were like parcels of dynamite. It could explode on your face, specially spreading its contents all around bringing to naked eye the oppression and enslavement of women in our own Modern age. As Keki Daruwalla rightly says, "The intensity of feeling, ably controlled in her better poems, and the uninhibited manner in which she treated sex, immediately won for her a big audience. Kamala Das is pre-eminently a poet of love and pain, one stalking the other through a near neurotic world. There is an all pervasive sense of hurt throughout. Love, the lazy animal hungers of the flesh, hurt and humiliation are the wrap and woof of her poetic fabric. She seldom ventures outside tins personal world."[2] In fact, she goes diving deep into her own self, unravelling mysteries which were never known to Indian women, or more honestly speaking, none dared to unravel them in the past, in such a away, in such an orthodox, custom-ridden, conservative society. Such poems, would have been burnt down had she lived half a century ago and dared to write the stuff she writes now. Bruce King is right when he writes, "Das's themes go beyond *stereotyped* longings and complaints. Even her feelings of loneliness and disappointments are part of a longer than life personality obsessive in its awareness of its self, yet creating; a drama of selfhood."[3]

She can never persuade her to forget that she is a woman, who craves for love, companionship and understanding. When she published her poems, "on the one hand it produced derisive laughter but on the other, more scholarly people often appreciated it as a maiden effort of an Indian woman to express herself without much inhibition circumscribed by the false and hypocritical rules of a conservative society."[4]

A closer look at her poems will show that love, sex, marriage and companionship were important subjects to her. Hari Mohan Prasad and Chandra Prasad Singh have understood these points clearly when they write,

> "Her poetry has often been considered as a gimmick in sex or striptease in words, an over exposer of body or 'snippets of trivia.' But the truth is that her poetry is an autobiography, an articulate voice of her ethnic identity, her Dravidian culture. In her, the poet is the poetry fully obliterating Eliot's distinction between the man suffering and the mind creating 'A poet's raw material,' she says, is not stone or clay; it is her personality. I could not escape from my predicament even for a moment."[5]

She wrote her poetry, on her own self discovering and expressing the different layers of hypocrisy, which got overcoated in our day today life. But she was bitterly criticised for that by the high priests of social morality. Her ideolistic ideas of love and domesticity became a casualty of rash criticism, for which she was not fully prepared .

While she finds it difficult to adjust to the barrenness of a married life, her childhood experiences and little joys sustains her in the cities. According to Bruce King the hollowness of her adult life is always overshadowed by the innocence of her childhood. There is a possible contrast between the village life and the city life in many of her poems. Her grand-mother is in her inner mind some kind of a complex which gives her the strength to face the realities of life. The sense of loss, depravity, alienation and superficiality get submerged under the 'yellow green pond' of her native village. She becomes sensitive the demands of active life, and its needs.

> "I know I have a life
> To be lived, and each nameless
> Corpuscle in me, has its life."
>
> (*Quoted in Bruce King*, p. 151)

She feels repelled against the existence under the burden of sickening experiences of her later life. But life is always interesting and it has to be lived. Her recollections from childhood affords a soothing effect. Bijay Kumar Das says in this connection,

> "Very often it is noted she leans heavily on her memory (and her grand-mother and her old house come alive) and from thereon she leaps on to a new subject in the poem. Thus, the past she recounts may be seen as a symbol of old human ties. Placed alongside with the present where she is searching for love, the past recalled throws light on the contemporary values."[6]

She often feels that love is a hollow word as the male dominated society, shows no understanding of a woman's aspirations,

> "...Why should I remember or bear
> That sweet sounding name, pinned to
> Me, a medal, undeservingly
> Gained at moments when, all of
> Me is ablaze with life?"
>
> (*Quoted in Bruce King*, p. 151)

Bruce King further says,

> "If many poems speak of unhappiness and the desire for an all absorbing love, others are filled with Das's discovery of the life around her on the streets and in the bedrooms. While marriage has hurt her ego, leaving her unfulfilled, her poems also record a woman enjoying the newness of the world as she wanders the streets and pursues her own interests."

She feels frustrated about her freedom that her husband offered her, when she got married. She expected a husband as understanding, as caring and as authoritative as her grandmother who looked after her, corrected and advised her. It was a matter of disappointment when her husband told her :

"You may have freedom,
as much as you want,
My soul balked at this diet of ash
Freedom became my dancing shoe
how well I danced
and danced without rest,
Until the shoes turned grimy on my feet,
and I began to have doubts."

(*Composition*)

The idea continues with more clarity in her poem "Substitute":

"End it, I cried, end it and let us be free
This freedom was our last strange toy
Like the hangman's robe, even while new,
It could give no pride. Nor even joy.
We kissed and we loved, all in a hurry
For another short hour or two
We went all warm and wild and lovely."

Throughout her writing career she searches for love; genuine and understanding love.

> "When she thinks of her freedom and life without checks, the memory of that house at Nalapat comes back to her as a soothing thought. She dreams of that house and thinks of going there and listening to the frozen air and bringing an armful of darkness to lie behind her bedroom like a "brooding dog, probably to keep a watch on her. The very thought of that house at Malabar created a sort of energy in her and an inspiration to live and love."[8]

But when she realizes that it is far away from her ancestral home in Malabar, in some far off city, it produces a sense of loss, frustration and a sense of torture in her. In her poem "A Hot Noon in Malabar" she writes in this respect :

"....Yes, this is
A noon for wild men, wild thoughts wild love. To
Be here, far away, is torture. Wild feet
Stirring up the dust, this hot noon, at my
Home in Malabar, I so far away...."

In far away barren cities where people neither love nor care each other; she spent her time counting the stars. She could not adjust to the new environs, which did not bother to give her love or kindness. Her husband "...who neither loved nor used her." In such a situation, probably she turned to other men, yearning for love, affection and caring. She writes,

"They did this to her, the men who knew her, the man
She loved, who loved her not enough, being selfish
And a coward, the husband who neither loved nor
Used her, but was a ruthless watcher, and the band
Of cynics she turned to, clinging to their chests where
New hair sprouted like great-winged moths,
burrowing her
Face into their smells and their young lusts to forget,
To forget, oh, to forget...and they said, each of
Them, I don't love, I cannot love, it is not
In my nature to love, but I can be kind to you...."

(*The Sunshine Cat*)

Her search for love and kindness ends up in a barren wasteland, where there is neither life nor hope. She spends her life in agony and frustrations, repenting and weeping most of the time.

"They let her slide from pegs of sanity into
A bed made soft with tears and she lay there weeping
For sleep had lost its use; I shall build walls with tears,
She said, walls to shut me in.... Her husband shut her
In every morning; locked her in a room of books...."

(*The Sunshine Cat*)

She had dreams of a loving husband who could provide her the bliss of a paradise. Instead, she feels the heat of a funeral pyre with her head constantly burning. She writes in her poem, "The Invitations,"

> ".... As long
> As I remember, I want no other.
> On the bed with him, the boundaries of
> Paradise had shrunk to a mere
> Six by two and afterwards, when we walked
> Out together, they
> Widened to hold the unknown city....
> End me, cries the sea. Think of yourself
> Lying on a funeral pyre
> With a burning head."

It is these frustrations which tempt her to commit suicide. 'The invitation' is from the sea to "Bathe cool, stretch your limbs on cool, Secret sands, pillow your head on anemones."

It is, therefore, clear that, "her romantic ideas about love and home have been shattered by an insensitive husband and the cries to whom she turned for love. Her husband hurt her feelings and evoked a sense of disappointment in her. The very first attempt that he made to express his love and affection towards her, produced a negative emotion in her."[9]

This point has been dealt in detail in her autobiography, *My Story*,

> "Before I left for Calcutta, my relative (her future husband) pushed me into a dark corner behind a door and kissed me sloppily near my mouth. He crushed my breasts with his thick fingers. I felt hurt and humiliated. All I said was a goodbye."[10]

> "This 'goodbye' assumes significance when one considers her alienation from her husband in later years after their marriage. Though basically he was not a bad man Kamala Das could not like him whole-heartedly. One of the reasons, though only psychological was that he was a close relative and they grew up together. She, it seems admired him as a friend and almost as a brother. But the sudden change of roles to bride and bridegroom was a little beyond her imaginations."[11]

She has also given graphic accounts of her relations with him, before their marriage right from her early childhood. From the following account of her relations with him in the early days, one can understand the embarrassment that she felt when he behaved differently and showed interest in her as a woman.

> Her admiration for the man is clear, but it doesn't show glimpses of her love and affection as a man or as a lover. In *My Story*, she has given expression to her ideas of an ideal lover. She writes,
>
> "I had expected him to take me in his arms and stroke my face, my hair, my hands, and whisper loving words. I had expected him to be all that I wanted my father to be, and my mother. I wanted conversation, companionship and warmth. Sex was far from my thoughts. I had hoped that he would remove with one sweep of his benign arms, the loneliness of my life."[12]

She, further, feels unhappy about her marriage, as she appeared to be a puppet and the strings of which being held firmly by her parents. She had no freedom in selecting an ideal lover for her. Others did all the planning for her marriage and she was not even consulted on the subject, leave alone, their trying to know about her prefer. In her own words, "My life had been planned and its course charted by my parents and relatives."[13] What hurt her most was this indifference to her individuality from her relations. As a modern woman she never liked the way in which they moved about and fixed as important an affair as her marriage without, even trying to know her ideas and aspirations. This attitude of her relations actually spoilt her life, according to her and she considered herself a helpless victim :

> "I was a victim of a youngman's carnal hunger and perhaps out of our union, there would be born a few children."[14]

This sense of helplessness and alienation prompts her to become a rebel and she looks down upon all her relations with contempt and disgust.

> "... Marriage meant, nothing more than a show of wealth to families like ours."[15]

Her alienation from her husband was complete with the type of experience she had from her husband immediately after her marriage with him. She writes, "Again and again he hurt me and all the while the Kathakali drums throbbed fully."[16] Another very interesting experience which put her off from him was her husband's extra marital affairs with another lady, leaving her alone, a virgin in her home. "Again she says she remained a virgin for a fortnight after marriage while he was after some other lady."[17] It is but natural that all her softer emotions were completely switched off, towards her husband. She writes about her husband,

"... his mouth, a dark
Cavern, where stalactites of
Uneven teeth gleam, his right
Hand on my knee, while our minds
Are willed to race towards love;
But they only wander, tripping
Idly over puddles of
Desire, can't this man with
Nimble finger-tips, unleash,
Nothing more alive than the
Skins lazy hungers? Who can
Help us who have lived so long
And have failed in love."

(*The Freaks*)

It is, therefore, clear that she feels crazy, hungry and unhappy, in the absence of true love in her life. She remained all through her life searching for love and understanding, which could not get even in little coins. Her heart, she says, remained, unfulfilled. She writes,

".... Who can
Help us who have lived so long,
And have failed in love? The heart,
An empty cistern waiting
Through long hours, fills itself
With coiling stakes of silence...
I am a freak."

(*The Freaks*)

She herself admits here that she is a freak. It can be sarcastical and in a sense of irony. But it is true that the companionship that she needed to unburden her agony her complaints and ungratefulness of children, she could never find in men for that you needed a patient mother, a sister or daughter by your side. She writes on this subject in her poem "The Female of the species,"

> "Sometimes you want to talk
> about love and despair,
> and ungratefulness of children,
> A man is no use whatever then
> You want then your mother
> Or sister
> Or the girl with whom you went through school,
> and your first love, and her
> first child-a girl-
> and your second."

(*The Female of the species*)

The feminine psychology and her needs, according to her can not be met by any man. He has got no time to sit with her and talk about the supposed anger, anguish and ambitions of a woman. Her life is more leisurely and she needs understanding and love; affections and care.

> "Kamala Das's story is the story of a woman who was denied love, when she valued nothing but love in all her life. Love and affection remained a craze, a longing and a dream for her. She got almost every thing in life name and fame, a degree of wealth but she could never get love, as she saw it. It is in this background that she writes about love in all her writings."[18]

It is this psychology of the feminine mind which gets its *focus* in her poems. For a woman, love is the essence of her life. The early flirtations, the teenage turbulance, the lust and sexual needs of the young woman, her love and affection for the children, the earing for the suffering and the concern for the unlucky; these are all nothing but the external expressions of her love. A woman craves for love and this love is not one-sided. She longs to receive love and to give love. Kamala Das found a desert in her life, and Saleem Peeradina has vividly stated this in the following statements, ably divided into categories,

> "She writes about love with the obsessiveness of a woman who can realize her being fully only through love.
>
> Not surprisingly, given the subject, the writing is sometimes weak and self-indulgent. Ah, why does love come to me like pain again and again and again?"
>
> (*The Testing of the sirens*)

Sometimes theatrical;

> "When I die
> Do not throw the meat and bones away
> But pile them up
> And
> Let them Tell
> By their smell
> What life was worth
> On this earth
> What love was worth
> In the end"
>
> (*A Request*)[19]

In her poems love is depicted in various forms, more often than not, the sterile aspect of it, the absence of love and the deprivation of it, by the society, by the relations and by the cultural traditions and customs. Peeradina writes further,

> "But in her poems, it is impossible not to be moved by and involved in the passionate urge and drive of the rhythm, the haunting images of sterility (Dance of the Eunuchs), the ultimate resilience in the face of any relationship that threatens to devastate her vital and potential self:
>
> "You called me wife
>
> I was taught to break saccharine into your tea and
> To offer at the right moment the vitamins cowering

Beneath your monstrous ego, I ate the magic loaf
and Became a dwarf."[20]

(*The Old Play House*)

Love also takes occasionally a woman to steal a moment of love in the company of a friend, as she writes,

"I must
Drive fast to town and
Lie near my friend for an hour"

(*The Joss-Sticks at Cadell Road*)

Often she is frightened to think about the loss of a man whom she loved. Loving, according to her is easy, to live without him later with his memory is hard for any woman.

"Getting a man to love you is easy.
Only be honest about your wants as
Woman ....
Oh, yes, getting
A man to love is easy, but living
Without him afterwards may have to be
Faced. A living without life when you move.
Around, meeting strangers, with your eyes that
Gave up their search, with ears that hear only
His last voice calling out your name and your
Body which once under his touch had gleamed
Like burnished brass, now drab and destitute."

(*Looking Glass*)

Often she becomes bitterly ironic and consoles herself by saying,

"It will be all right if I put up my hair,
Stand near my husband to make a proud pair..."

(*Substitute*)

"Thus, one can see that there is a search for security, understanding, shelter and a happy home. Love always meant something more than physical to her. What she actually wanted from her husband was sympathy, understanding and companionship. She has lived all her life in search of illusive love and company."[21]

The complexity of her mind and her ideas, cannot be easily understood by common man. The pulls and pushes of cultural restrictions, family background and the traditions of an orthodox family have often shaped her feelings and ideas, often confusing, often outspoken, but never timid and surrendering.

Bruce King is right when he writes :

> "...the poems of Kamala Das when focused on love, treat it within a broader changes of themes, more realized settings and with deeper feelings, bringing to it an intensity of emotion and speech and a rich, full complexity of life."[22] He further says, "Das's themes go beyond stereotyped longings and complaints. Even her feelings of loneliness and disappointments are part of a larger-than-life personality, obsessive in its awareness of itself, yet creating a drama of selfhood."[23]

III

Discovery of Self and Sexuality

The discovery of self and sexuality in Kamala Das's poetry are connected. She was the product of the modern age and according critics modern age is *synonymous* with Indian Renaissance. There is a belief that European Renaissance tempted people to travel fast into strange distant worlds, while Indian Renaissance led them straight into their own self. I.K. Sharma, has also expressed the same idea when he writes,

> "The greatest gift of the Renaissance in Europe, it is said, is the discovery of America. The search for the new, the hunger for the unknown, finally led the Europeans to its shore. The greatest gift of the Indian Renaissance, on the other hand, is the discovery of the self."[24]

Indo-Anglian poetry, started off as a new branch, somewhat like a hide and seek, a sort of writing which they thought would be caught and exposed, or was written with a guilty feeling or an apology that they were writing in a foreign language. It was like traditional Hindu boy marrying, a foreign white girl who didn't bother about Indian culture and tradition. Therefore, these poets generally took shelter under Indian Epics or religion-oriented subjects. Some others pretending to be more liberal and modern embraced philosophy and mysticism. Hardly, any one opened up their minds and looked into it. "Their vertical vision had enough music and colour, strength and affection. But they rarely spoke with their hearts inside out."[25]

Ezekiel, another Indo-Anglian, poet is famous to refer to his surroundings and to manipulate the reader to understand the world, which he wants them to see : Kamala Das is different; altogether different. As Bruce King says,

> "Das opened areas, in which previously forbidden or ignored emotions could be expressed in ways which reflect the true voice of feeling. She showed how an Indian woman poet could create a space for herself in the public world. She brings a sense of locality to her poems. There are rooms in which she lives, homes she has left, the bedrooms, restaurants and streets in which she meets her lovers, the rides in cars, the people she visits or notices, the people she addresses in personal terms. Whereas Ezekiel consciously refers to the environments. Das's poems assume their locations create their space by being set in situations rather than observing or alluding to their environments."[26]

Kamala Das, in her effort to discover, her own self, unknowingly shook the norms of a male dominated society, which continued its existence through hundreds of years, with very little changes she has crossed all limits permitted for a society lady. I.K. Sharma has worked out two sets of words from her poems to find the meaning of them. The first set of words reveal the whole world of women along with their cultural paraphernalia :

> "Marriage, wedding drums, bedrooms, bride bouquet double bed, pillow, mirrors, bangles, bells, gems, sandalscent, musk, dolls, lipstick, perfumes, oils, breast, flesh, mouth, lick, lips kiss, embrace, love, lust, honeymoon, hair, pigtails, legs, heart, womb,

spittle, pubis"[27] and a lot more. She looks into the minds of women and express their worlds for us.

She says,

> The tragedy of life
> is not death but growth ...."

(*Composition*)

What she means by "growth" is not the growth of a girl into adulthood or a woman alone. Her "growth" is nothing but the growth of a girl into a wife and mother. We are in the habit of thinking from the male point of view. But hers is a steady and strong female vision. As I.K. Sharma says, "Put together, her poetry is a dissertation and that too a well documented one ...."[28]

Her experiences, as expressed through her poems have been unkind and unadorable type. Her experiences are of isolation, turbulance and depression.

He has given another set of words, that lay scattered in her poems, which are ungenteel and may offend the sophisticated tastes. The words are,

> "bone, skeleton, burning, halfburnt, mosques, X-ray rooms, dark caverns, tomb, pyre, bier, mire, garbage, burial, corpsebearers, mourners, fire, ash, cool, cutter, black veil lesbian, hetero, frigid, urine, cabaret, poison, eunuchs, convicts, murder, blood-stain, menstrual blood, rabid, schizophrenia eczema, mildew, arthritis, ischemia, anaemia, illness, death, hacking, virus, etc."[29]

One set of words are representative of childhood, innocence and host of words connected with feminine-life like lipstick, marriage and bangles, while the next list speaks of death, decay, and dark caverns. In his opinion all her poems stand in tension between these two sets and that, in fact, is the soul of her poems. She brings in her childhood memory into her poems. I.K. Sharma further says in this connection,

> "Very often it is noted, she leans heavily on her memory (and her grand-mother and her old house come alive) and from thereon she leaps on to a new subject in the poem. Thus, the past she recounts

> may be seen as symbol of old human ties. Placed alongside with the present where she is searching for love, the past recalled throws light on the contemporary values."[30]

This contrast between the present and the past, happiness with unhappiness, life with decay, childhood with the adulthood continues in her poems. As Albert Mordel says, "works of imagination open up to the reader hidden vistas in man's inner life just as dreams do. In Kamala Das this opening of the hidden vistas forms the matrix of her entire poetry."[31] She, though is classified alongwith Sylvia Plath, Anne Sexton and Judith Wright and noted for the confessional mode of writing. Such poets normally take shelter under mysticism and hysterias. In her case it is not true.

> "Her poetry has often been considered as a gimmick in sex or striptease in words, an over-exposer of body or 'Snippets of trivia.' But the truth is that her poetry is an autobiography, an articulate voice of her ethnic identity, her Dravidian culture. In her the poet is the poetry fully obliterating *Eliot's* distinction between the man suffering and the mind creating." A poet's raw material, she says, "is not stone or clay; it is her personality. I could not escape from my predicament even for a moment."[32]

IV

A Feminist Poetess

Feminism, is like a new missile often fired at any modern woman writer. The evolution of the term itself is interesting. In countries like America and England where women enjoy a lot of freedom and social status went to the extreme extent of even abusing men, just for the fun and publicity that it afforded to them. Its echoes were heard mildly in India.

The conditions in India are quite contradictory and confusing. Women are placed on a pedestal and worshipped on the one hand and treated badly and enslaved on the other. Indian women were happy to live in the four walls of the house, looking after the kitchen and the children. Conditions were not better in Europe also in the last century. In his poem "The Princess" Tennyson has written,

"Man for the field and woman for the hearth
Man for the sword and for the needle she
Man to command and woman to obey"[33]

The Industrial Revolution, brought about a change in Europe, while the Indian concept remained the same. In the nineteenth century woman started working in Europe making themselves less dependent on men. As a result woman started asserting their position and fighting for their rights. This movement is termed as "Feminism." Feminism did not get a lot of importance in India. But still, its effects are seen in some of the films and writings. It is not that there are no problems for women in India. In fact, women suffer a lot, especially, in the rural areas at the hands of men. But still women fight within a certain limits only in India. The main area where Indian women concentrated their activity was to bring in sanity to customs and traditions like 'sati,' by which women were burned to death on the pyres of their husbands. Such an action was treated with pomp and ceremony, with the sanction of religion, thereby, denying the basic right for life to women. It is such customs and traditions, which enslave women, which have to be fought against.

Kamala Das, is generally seen in the fore-front of such writers who fought for the rights of women. She found it difficult to maintain her family relations. The most loved family member to her was her grand-mother. She wanted her father's affection and love. But she didn't get it the way she wanted it. She writes in her poem, "Next to Indira Gandhi,"

"Father, I ask you now without fear
Did you want me
Did you ever want a daughter
Did I disappoint you much
With my skin as dark as yours,"[34]

She then continues

"You chose my clothes for me
My tutors, my hobbies, my friends,
And at fifteen with my first saree you picked
me a husband."[35]

She further says,

"But it was not the right most grove for me
It wasn't my cup of tea"[36]

About the marriage she has expressed her disappointment time and again to tell the world that women are not mere toys, they are also individuals with their own preferences. She is not a toy to be kept beside a man to be married. She writes about her marriage

"It was never a husband and wife bond,
We were such a Mismatched pair"[37]
......

"He was like a bank locker
Steely cold and shut
Or a filing cabinet that
Only its owner could unlock
Not for a moment did I own him"[38]

One comes across the soul of Kamala Das, struggling and at the same time asserting her own existence and her own individuality in all her poems. But at the same time her revulsion, her irony, her disappointments were never swept under the carpets.

Her dissatisfaction is clear from the lines from "The old play House"

".... you were pleased
with my body's response, its weather, its usual shallow,
Convulsions. You dribbled spittle in to my mouth, you poured
Yourself into every every nook and cranny you embalmed
My poor lust with your bitter sweet juices ... . covering
Beneath your monstrous ego, I ate the magicloaf and
became a dwarf. I lost my will and reason, to all your
questions, I mumbled in coherent replics"[39]

The quest for emotional rapport and her failure to establish a meaningful relationship with others, whether it is her husband, the society or the members of her family is the burden of her poetry. In her poem 'The suicide' she writes,

"I must pose
I must pretend

I must act the role
Of happy woman
Happy wife"[40]

She would have been satisfied with love and understanding from her husband. She writes,

"But a sunny porch and my husband beside me alive,
That is all that I would ask for
In my old age
I shall retire from youth without a murmur,
Fold up my lust neatly like a wedding gown
Put it away for good."[41]

Confessional Poet

Kamala Das is often grouped under the group confessional poets. She has succeeded in going into the subconscious needs, desires and aspirations of the feminine mind. Anisur Rahman comments in this connection, "As a poet, she explores her psychic geography with an exceptional female energy and achieves the capability to express her inimitable vision through the technique of sincerity."[42]

Some world famous poets in the confessional mode are Robert Lowell, Theodore Roethke, Anne Sexton, John Berryman and Sylvia Plath. Sylvia Plath is often compared with Kamala Das. She was also emotionally and socially upset and she committed suicide at the young age of thirty. She wrote poetry which had profound insights into the inner depths of human minds.

Kamala Das also shared some of the qualities of Sylvia Plath, like her suicidal tendencies.

Kamala Das's poem "The suicide" is specially, significant in this connection she writes :

"O sea, I am fed up
I want to be simple
I want to be loved
And
If love is to be had
I want to be dead, just dead"[43]

While Sylvia Plath writes,

"Dying
Is an art, like everything else,
I do it exceptionally well"[44]

These two poets have quite a number of points in common and is a topic for detailed study.

V

Conclusion

In conclusion one can easily see that Kamala Das is a modern, Indo-Anglian poet, who is highly sensitive and feminine. She found herself in a custom ridden, orthodox society dominated by men who looked different and acted different. They looked funny, repulsive, self-centered and proud to Kamala Das : Women on the other hand are dolls in the hands of men. She could not adjust herself to this situation and, therefore, she highlighted the sensitivity of her mind through her poems. According to her, modern women need freedom, self respect and they are prepared to shoulder responsibility. Her poems are a vehicle to bring out the suppressed tension in the minds of women, who are reluctant to speak, unlike Kamala Das. Kamala Das, therefore, has expressed her emotions freely through her poems, making herself, controversial and at the same time world famous.

REFERENCES

1. Bruce King. *Modern Poetry in English* (OUP, Bombay, 1987) : 147.
2. Keki N. Daruwalla. *Two Decades of Indian Poetry*, Vikas Publishing House, Ghaziabad, 1980.
3. Bruce King.
4. O.J. Thomas. "Kamala Das : A Search for Home, Companionship and Love," *The Quest*, Vol. V (June, 1991) : 28.
5. Harimohan Prasad and Chandra Prasad Singh (ed.). *Indian Poetry in English* (New Delhi : Sterling Publications, 1985) : 35.
6. Bijay Kumar Das. *Contemporary Indo-English Poetry* (Bareilly : Prakash Book Depot, 1986) : 47.
7. King, 151.
8. Thomas, 31.
9. Thomas.

10. Kamala Das. *My Story*, Sterling Publications, New Delhi, 1976, Preface.
11. Thomas.
12. Thomas 87.
13. K. Das, *My Story*. 88.
14. Das 90.
15. Das.
16. Das 92.
17. Thomas 32.
18. Thomas 34.
19. Saleem Peeradina. *Contemporary Indian Poetry in English*, (Madras : Macmillan, 1972) : 85.
20. Peeradina 86.
21. Thomas 34
22. Bruce King 147.
23. King.
24. I.K. Sharma. "The Irony of six : A study of Kamala Das's poetry" in Bijay Kumar Das (ed.) *Contemporary Indo-English Poetry* (Bareilly : Prakash Book Depot, 1986) : 41.
25. Sharma 42.
26. King 152 to 153.
27. Sharma 42.
28. Sharma 43.
29. Sharma 44.
30. Sharma 47.
31. Hari Mohan Prasad and C.P. Singh. *Indian Poetry*. 35.
32. Prasad and Singh
33. Alfred Tennyson. "The Princess," *Alfred Tennyson Selected Poems* (ed.). A.N. Dwivedi (Delhi, 1985) : 34.
34. Kamala Das. "Next Indira Gandhi," *Only the soul knows How to sing,*" D.C. Books (Kottayam : DC Books, 1996) : 118.
35. Das.
36. Das.
37. Kamala Das. "Larger than life." Das 112.
38. Das.
39. Das.
40. Das 86.
41. Kamala Das. "Daughter of the Century." Das 131.
42. Anisur Rahman. *Expressive form in the Poetry of Kamala Das* (Abhinav Publications, 1981) : 1.
43. Kamala Das. *Only the soul knows to sing*. 87.
44. Sylvia Plath, Lady Lizarus, Richard Clay, in *The Penguin Book of American verse* (Chancer Press Ltd., 1986) : 573.

5

Body And Beyond : Love Poetry of Kamala Das

P. MALLIKARJUNA RAO*

Kamala Das lends a new dimension to her love poetry by revealing her kinship with an anterior Indian tradition which has its roots in Indian epics. Apart from this, her Nayar background not only provides a suitable background but also strengthens the confessional streak of her poetry. Thus the significant aspect of her love poetry is the merger of two traditions — the Indian and the Western. It is in this light that an attempt is made here to examine Kamala Das' love poetry.

Search for love is the principal preoccupation of Kamala Das' poetry. She confesses with utmost candour that she "began to write poetry with the ignoble aim of wooing a man."[1] As a result love becomes the pervasive theme and it is through love that she endeavours to discover herself. As she concerns herself with various facets of love, her love poetry can be divided into two phases. While in the first phase her obsessive concern with physical love is quite prominent, in the second, her drift towards ideal love can be discerned. By ideal love she means the kind of relation that exists between the legendary Radha and Krishna. She yearns for such a love which does not impede her impulse to freedom. Her concept of ideal love is embedded in the poem "The Old Playhouse."

... Love is Narcissus at the waters' edge, haunted
By its own lovely face, and yet it must seek at last

*Department of English, Kakatiya University, Warangal.

An end, a pure, total freedom, it must will the mirrors
To shatter and the kind night to erase the water.

In the narcissistic phase, the lovers do not outgrow their egos which stand as hurdles preventing their merger. They are chained in self-admiration. But it is not a permanent phase as it undergoes mutations seeking "total freedom." It is in the second phase of ideal love that the lovers transgress the boundaries of their egos or narrow selves to merge with each other, as such merger ensures total freedom. The poet beholds such an exemplary relation in the love between Radha and Krishna. She surmises herself as Radha who goes in search of Krishna, the ideal lover, in spite of her marriage. This brings into her poetic context the *Abhisarika* tradition of Sanskrit poetry.[2] Besides this her uninhibited treatments of love and sex reminds one of *Sahaja* tradition.[3]

But in Kamala Das the element of *bhakti* is absent. Her relation with Krishna is purely human. She confesses, "I was looking for an ideal lover. I was looking for the one who went to Mathura and forgot to return to his Radha."[4] Thus the poet lives simultaneously in two worlds, the actual world, where love usually is a synonym for lust, in her words "skin communicated love," and the mythical world of Vrindavan.

While there is so much in her poetry which seems to draw from earlier Indian traditions, there are also various shades of physical love described in the confessional mode. This mode of expression, suits her as she ventilates her personal experiences and humiliations and also the intensity of her experience. In conformity with the confessional tradition, she talks in poetic terms about her unpleasant sexual experiences. Inevitably her poems are autobiographical. This lends a kind of authenticity to her poetry which is found lacking in much of love poetry written today. She says, "A Poet's raw material is not stone or clay; it is her personality."[5] Hence, the emotional and sexual traumas she experiences become the subject matter of her poems. In the initial stages she submits herself to sexual desires and pleasures : "now here is a girl with vast/sexual hungers/a bitch after my own heart." She is not ashamed to call herself a bitch. Marriage comes as a disappointment to her for "in the orbit of licit sex, there seemed to be only crudeness and violence."[6] This failure to get love within the framework of marriage leads her to seek it outside wedlock.

"... beg now at strangers' doors to/Receive love, at least in small change?"

But very soon she realizes the futility of her search. She finds the remedy worse than the disease. For instance, when she fails to receive love from her husband, she turns to a "band of cynics." But "they said, each of/Them, I do not love, I cannot love, it is not/In my nature to love, but I can be kind to you ...." What she needs is not kindness but love. They only toy with her body and do not fulfil her psychic needs. They assuage the "skin's lazy hungers" with a violence and primitiveness described in "Convicts." "That was the only kind of love, /This hacking at each other's parts/Like convicts hacking breaking clods, /At noon." Such talking about one's personal humiliation is typical of a confessional poet. So to save her face she would.

"... flaunt, at/Times, a grand flamboyant lust." And consequently, "With a cheap toy's indifference" she enters other's Lives, and makes every trap of lust "A temporary home."

The agony of not finding a true lover and a sense of defeat oppress her and she finds no way out of this limbo of sex. She becomes aware of the fact that reliance on body cannot carry her far enough and it is a trap which prevents her from experiencing true love.

As the convict studies
His prison's geography
I study the trappings
Of your body, dear love,
For I must some day find
An escape from its snare.

(The Prisoner)

She discovers that, after all, the pleasures body offers are of cloying and ephemeral nature. A love which flourishes and thrives on body is bound to wither with it and the search for true love in a world of philanderers is a futile exercise. So she turns to the mythical world of Krishna and Vrindavan to seek lasting love and fulfilment. She imagines herself as Radha and finds comfort in the arms of imaginary Krishna. Further she can experience absolute liberty from the rigid social code and the constraints of super ego in the presence of Krishna. In psychological terms, Krishna, as Sudhir Kakar remarks, "encourages the individual to identify with an ideal primal self, released from all social and super ego constraints. Krishna's promise, like that of Dionysus in ancient Greece, is one of utter freedom and instinctual exhilaration."[7] Contrary to her husband's love which cribs and confines her, Krishna promises total freedom.

Her grandmother's younger sister Ammalu, also a poet, exerted a positive influence on Kamala Das. She was a worshipper of Krishna and wrote several poems in His praise. Though she was pretty and eligible, she remained a spinster until her death. She was very faithful to Lord Krishna and in her last poem she wrote, "My chastity is my only gift to you, Oh, Krishna..." Her writings seem to have "disturbed" Kamala Das very much.

The haunting image of Krishna becomes inseparable. She remembers him on her bridal night and when she is pregnant and also while playing with her son. He appears to her in "myriad shapes" and resides in her consciousness : "... whose blue face is/ A phantom-lotus on the waters of my dreams."

During onc of the bouts of her illness, she has a mystical experience. While the fear of death grips her heart, she hears "a low whistling ... that sounded like the playing of a flute...."[8]

It is against this background that one can appreciate the significance of her Krishna poems. "Ghanshyam" depicts vividly the transformation that was wrought in her by her relentless search for love. She realizes that her husband can never establish a rapport with her soul, because "And each time his lust was quietened/And he turned his back on me ..." What she seeks is a total merger in her lover. But since it is not feasible in the actual world, she searches for Ghanshyam, the ideal lover. Dissolution of the individual self and the total identification is possible only with her mythical lover. This is illustrated by the poem "Radha," where she somewhat sentimentally depicts the ecstasy Radha experiences in Krishna's embrace. She cries :

> Everything in me
> is melting, even the hardness at core
> O, Krishna, I am melting, melting, melting

Nothing remains but
you ...

But Radha does not snap her marital ties in spite of her love for Krishna as she considers her corporeal form insignificant. She is contemptuous of her husband who only wants the warmth of her body. The poem entitled "Maggots" embodies Radha's experience with her husband which is analogous to the predicament of the poet. Radha does not experience rapture in the arms of her husband, but remains as a corpse, indifferent.

At sunset, on the river bank, Krisna
Loved her for the last time and left...
That night in her husband's arms, Radha felt
So dead that he asked, what is wrong
Do you mind my kisses, love? And she said,
No, not at all, but thought, what is
It to the corpse if the maggots nip?

(Maggots)

Thus Krishna has a therapeutic role to play in the poet's life. Her thoughts about Him give her relief from the asphyxiating male chauvinism. Another woman poet who wrote on Krishna was Sarojini Naidu. Her collection of poems *The Feather of Dawn* contains a section entitled Krishna poems. It will be interesting to contrast Kamala Das's treatment of Krishna motif with that of Sarojini Naidu.

In her poem "Ghanshyam" Sarojini Naidu depicts Krishna not as her lover but as God who is omniscient and omnipotent and is the central principle of this universe.

Thou givest to the shadows on the mountains
The colours of thy glory, Ghanshyam
Thy laughter to high secret snow-fed mountains,
To forest pines thy healing breath of balm.
Thou lendest to the storm's unbridled tresses
The beauty and blackness of thy hair...

This poem is written in the form of *Stotraa* hymn in praise of God. The tone of the poem suggests the high seriousness of a devotee. She offers the lord not her body like Kamala Das but her "yearning soul"; "O take my yearning soul for thine oblation."

Kamala Das, on the other hand, considers Krishna as her "mate" who comes to her in "myriad forms" and to whom "In many shapes shall I surrender ... I shall be fondled by Him."[9]

In her "Songs of Radha," Sarojini Naidu describes the restlessness, anxiety and pain Radha experiences in waiting for her lover, Krishna. Her songs are rhythmic and have a musical appeal, while Kamala Das' poems are short, and highly personal. While spontaneity characterises Sarojini's poems, brooding and meditation permeate Kamala Das's poems. In Sarojini Naidu the Radha-Krishna relationship is a metaphor for that between *Atman* and *Brahman;* in Kamala Das the relationship, though one of ideal lovers, is realized in human terms, and as such it does not rise to "the divine level." Sarojini Naidu's Radha is not anti-sexual, yet sex is not the primary concern in the Radha poems. But in Kamala Das sex implies a "deep and intense relationship" which is not devotional; it is very much human in its concern. Fritz Blackwell rightly observes that the poet's "concern is literary and existential, not religious; she is using a religious concept for a literary motif and metaphor."[10]

Thus Kamala Das's love poems stand apart as they fruitfully combine the indigenous traditions such as *Abhisarika* and *Sahaja* and the confessional tradition which is Western. Her love poetry is a fine blending of the two different literary traditions.

REFERENCES

1. As quoted by K. Indrasena Reddy. *The Poetry of Kamala Das : A Study of Her Themes* (unpublished M. Phil. thesis), Kakatiya University, Warangal, 1981.

2. According to *Abhisarika* Tradition a woman goes to meet her lover braving elements, darkness etc. She is supposed to be Radha and her lover Krishna. Radha-Krishna relation is considered as metaphoric of *Atma-Brahman* relation.

3. Medieval *Sahaja* poet espoused free love as a means of self-realization. Kamala Das's discussion of her emotional and sexual traumas with exceptional candour reminds R. Parthasarathy of *Sahaja* tradition. Ref. R. Parthasarathy, "Tradition and Freedom," *The Indian Journal of English Studies*, 21 (1981-82) : 56.

4. Kamala Das. *My Story* (New Delhi : Sterling, 1976) : 191.

5. Das 74.

6. Das 33.

7. Sudhir Kakar, *The Inner World : A Psycho-analytic Study of Childhood and Society in India* (Delhi : Oxford, 1981) : 142.
8. Atma Ram, "An Interview with Kamala Das," *The Book Maker* 5, No. 6 (June 1978) : 1.
9. *My Story*; 208.
10. Fritz Blackwell, "Krishna Motifs in the Poetry of Sarojini Naidu and Kamala Das." *Journal of South Asian Literature* 13, Nos. 1-4 (1977-78) : 13.

6

The Onset of Poetic Rebellion : An Explication of Kamala Das's 'An Introduction'

JAYAKRISHNAN NAIR*

It is in the writings of Kamala Das that the Indian-English poetry acquired for itself a real substantity that matches equally with the creative contributions of the Western Confessionalists like Sylvia Plath and Anne Sexton of America. Of all the women poets of the present in India, Das projects herself as a fervent feminist poetic voice always exacting for a dignified place of honour, a respect for the naturalistic freedoms and choices. Her poetry contributes for the strong reactions and justifications for the most needful awakening of woman as a living entity in being-in-the world.

The modern Indian-English poetry with all its aggressiveness and boldness begins and culminates in Kamala Das. No other feminist poet in India could achieve the absolute rebellious dimensions of Kamala Das in her poetry. In fact, Kamala Das makes a poetic revolt by way of introspectively pondering upon the unfortunate state of existence in which Indian women conduct themselves. Like a seasonal artist she penetrates her imaginative potential to sympathetically understand the possible average grievances of Indian woman as extremely exploited agent in the social, domestic circumstances.

*Assistant Professor (English), Govt. Arts, Commerce and Science College, Khairagarh P.O. and Distt. Rajnandgaon.

This paper focuses on one of Kamala Das's earlier and most successful poems, 'An Introduction,' which marks her entry into the realm of Indian-English poetry with an unequivocal declaration of her poetic revolt. 'An Introduction' first appeared in her first collection of poems, 'Summer In Calcutta.' In 'An Introduction' the fission and fusion of different related themes within the framework of feminist cause, takes place with a cinematic effect. In fact, many of the thematic dimensions and variations of her poetry are sensitively and obliquely hinted in this poem. Therefore, it can be conjectured that 'An Introduction' is the most representative of her poetic genre, that is the exclusive feminist-rebellion.

Thematic concerns in Das's poetry range from the sad plight of woman in society, and the harrowing situations of feminine experiences to a longing for the freedom of the inner self through experiencing consummate love in the interpersonal relationships. However, she culminates her poetic journey with the note of a forced reconciliation, a realization of the pathetic nature of human situation. 'An Introduction' is an autobiographical initiation of her poetic verve wherein Kamala Das makes a categorical introspective exposition of an average woman-child in the process of her growth and development under oppressive and humiliating circumstances in our culture. The poem begins with the following statements:

> 'I don't know politics, but I know the names of
> those in power, and can repeat them like days of
> week, or names of months.'
>
> ('An Introduction,' *Summer In Calcutta*)

The use of antithesis in stating 'I don't know politics' and then asserting 'but I know the names of those in power, and can repeat them like days of week, or names of months' has its own purpose of ventilating the painful manner in which the 'politics' of man and woman-interpersonal relationships are creating a harrowing unrest in her introspective moments. The inalienable manner in which the politics of sex wounded her personality is substantially stated here. What goes in the poem hereafter is a continual resentment towards the politics of sex in the context of which woman arduously suffers a suffocatively inexpressible stance.

The manner in which Das substantiates her argument has the

poetic delicacy coupled with the stubbornness, expressing her 'angst.' This quality first finds expression in the argument on her poetic medium. She asks her 'friends,' 'critics' and 'visiting cousins' :

> 'Why not let me speak in
> Any language I like? The language I speak
> Becomes mine, its distortions, its queernesses,
> All mine, mine alone. It is half English, half
> Indian, funny perhaps, but it is honest,
> It is human as I am human, don't
> You see? and it is useful to me as cawing
> Is to crows or roaring to the lions it
> Is human speech.'
>
> ('An Introduction')

All this argumentation about the parameters of language here suggests at one simple point that any language cannot comprehend the intensity of her pain and agony. In this context, the poet's own words are worth quoting :

> "I don't find it easy to write either in English or in Malayalam. Language has been very difficult for me .... Thoughts were there, but to cover them up, to wrap them up in decent language is very difficult. I am discovering a new language, trying to make a new language, create it, which will suit me. Because I have yet to find a language which can keep pace with thinking."[1]

In creating her own language, Kamala Das surpasses all the possible linguistic conventions. In effect her 'All mind, mine alone' language is a violent formula of expressing the very heat and dust of her humiliation in being a sabotaged and relegated being in the world. It is interesting to note that all this heat and dust is directed towards the trenchant sexual politics ingrained in our social and domestic conventions.

'Cowing' of crows, and 'roaring' of lions are involuntary and instantaneous outcries of the occasions. Likewise, the human occasions in the volatile circumstances prompt such involuntary outcries in order to give vent to the pent-up repressed feelings and emotions. What the poet implies here is the fact that her poems are the proper outcries of the occasions. The pleasure and the pain of these 'cries' are inseparably involved. The love of expression on the one hand, and the agony of the expressed on the other, ultimately contribute for the sad outcries, *i.e.*, her poems. In this context, her poetry takes its life-blood from the British Romantics and the modern 'Confessionalists' who always insisted upon pain as the necessary spring-board of human expressions.

Kamala Das's 'outcries' are on the central ground of the painful experience of being a woman. What has stirred her sensitive psyche is the dehumanization of woman as a being. The spiralling self, as an insect pinned to a wall, rages within against this lack of social recognition for her lot. The articulation of this anger becomes impossible in any socially accepted language formulas. It has to be honest, and, therefore, it necessitates stretching of her

'two dimensional
Nudity on sheets of weeklies, monthlies,
Quarterlies, a sad sacrifice.'

('Loud Posters'— *Old Playhouse and Other Poems*)

Kamala Das is a self conscious poet, and does not pretend ignorance about her unique position as a feminist mouthpiece. This uniqueness is asserted when she says that her poems are :

'the speech of the mind
That is here and not there, a mind that sees and hears and
Is aware. Not the deaf, blind speech
Of trees in storm or of monsoon clouds or rain or the
Incoherent mutterings of the blazing Funeral pyre.

('An Introduction')

Vrinda Nabar complains of ambiguity in these lines, and asks :

> "What precisely do phrases like 'here and there' mean?...All this sounds suspiciously like raving, an extravagance."[2]

But a closer look at the context as brought out in the poem would reveal that there is no place for ambiguity or verbosity here. The 'mind that is here and not there' is a confident pronouncement of the originality of her poetic revolt. This originality is asserted through suggesting the spatial variation of the mind, the mind that is not to be found elsewhere. It is a hint at her resolution to override the traditional limits prescribed for the expositions of feminine psyche. Moreover, 'the deaf, blind speech of trees,' the 'monsoon clouds,' 'the rain,' and the 'mutterings' of the 'funeral pyre' are basically meaningless sound productions. These elements of Nature may have the ability of expression, but are free from suffocating experience of inexpressibility. Also since the dead do not know who died, the funeral pyres cannot subjectively lament the death. The poet's position is in contrast to that of these elements. In fact these lines have the effect of a sudden waking from a hallucinatory state of inexpressibility and suffocation, and bursting out. And at the background of this outburst is a rebellious spirit against centuries of oppression undergone by women.

'An Introduction' also deals with one of the major themes in Das's poetry — a lamentation for the lost innocence of childhood and its surroundings. In her poetry she very often recalls her grandmother's loving care to suggest the present lack of such an agent to console her. In a way she falls into loneliness and the introspection thereby turns out to be a painful confession of her concerns with life, particularly as woman in the Indian situation. Reference to her grandmother's protective love and affection and the later agony of loneliness that she feels, is also a concerned reflection at the wreck of the joint family system. When she was still a child, lying beside the grandmother at her ancestral (Nalappat) house, she —

'could hear at night
the surf breaking on the shore'

('Composition,' *The Descendants*)

The vastness of the sea symbolizes the extent of freedom that the poet longs for, which was well within her reach, both in its physical and abstract forms, under the warmth and care of the grandmother.

But 'That was long ago
Before the skin

intent on survival
learnt lessons of self-betrayal.'

('Composition')

Here is a clear indication that with the growth in age woman also develops a sense of growth in the instinctive demands. The expression 'skin intent on survival' is very significant. It is inevitable that the growth in age automatically brings forth certain instinctive desires. These desires were not prominent so long the grandmother took care of her. Ceasing of such a protective shade is the starting point of the skin's secret cherishings of new freedoms. The way she uses the expression 'survival' and not 'existence' confirms the force of creaturely demands in growth and development. There is no alternative freedom left for the creature in growth. The almost coercive manner in which the child gets distanced from its childhood's warmth and care is beautifully expressed in the lines :

'I was busy growing
I had then
No time for the sea'

('Composition')

The sea symbolizes the magnificent 'other' as against the self which is totally engrossed in its own properties of growth and development. The suggestion here is that when the self is totally pre-occupied with its own being, it does not have a relative vision of the 'other.' The sea also symbolizes the sea of life in the sense of the grand panoramic problematic nature of existence in the world. The self in its total pre-occupation with the concomitance of its own growth and growing demands, cannot concentrate on the 'other' as an entity available for its perusal. It precisely suggests the simple idea that when the instinctive urge predominates the self, the inevitable 'other' as a presence ceases to be operative. This irreversible course of alteration resulting in the irretrievable loss of a much better time is an agonizing experience for her, hence her resolution that :

'The tragedy of life is not death, but growth,
the child growing into adult,
and growing out of needs.'

('Composition')

Thus, it is rather the temporal distance than the spatial separation that is the cause of the nostalgic sentiments in Kamala Das. The root of every problem for her is the distinct phases of alteration and change from childhood to adolescence and then to womanhood. The relative manner in which she presents the various facets of growth in life ultimately contributes to one simple summation, that is life in its overall presentation of growth and development offers no relative comfort or ease. In all probability life has to be lived, and for the poet it has to be lived with all contingent regrets and distinct agonies from time to time. The manner in which she presents the agony of living ultimately matches with that of the Greek poets and philosophers who untiringly depicted life as a grim ironic presentation having no ease or respite from the pains of living. But she very often attempts a poetic retreat into the good old days as in 'My Grandmother's House' wherein she says :

> 'There is a house now far away where once
> I received love.
> ....
> ....You cannot believe, darling
> Can you, that I lived in such a house and was proud,
> and loved....
>
> ('My Grandmother's House,' *Summer In Calcutta*).

This kind of need for a regress into the childhood is a formal stylistic device in the Romantics and their followers, the 'Confessionalists.' It is rather their potential manner of expressing the painful undecided nature of being-in-the here-and-now. Being-in-the here-and-now is a matter of inordinate crisis and indecisiveness. The imaginative stress on the need for escape from the ardous nature of existing in the present into a childhood that might have been comparatively free from constraints, 18 a mere fib of poetic imagination. This escape, as cherished by Kamala Das, is just her own manner of poetically suggesting that the present is insufferable.

In 'An Introduction' this agony of growth is expressed but in an ironic tone :

> "I was child, and they

Told me I grew, for I became tall, my limbs
Swelled and one or two places sprouted hair.'

('An Introduction')

This physical change is but no ecstatic experience for her but is only a prelude to the onset of social and cultural complexities of adjustments. This alteration or growth is typically unadjustable because of its chaotic novelty conditioned to the pathetic reflection imposed by fellowmen and the family members.

She remains under constant threat of loss of the given. Life appears to be slipping out of the grips, like a fish that constantly slips out of the clutches of the fisher, in the sea of living. The dilemma that the poet projects reminds one of a child eating sweetmeat that wants to relish it and hold it back too.

Kamala Das is predominantly a poet of love. The all-pervasive spirit of the whole poetic world of hers is of love and its vigorous manifestations drawn from life-experiences, both exhilarating and agonizing. About the recurring love themes in Das's poetry. A.N. Dwivedi observes :

> "The frequency of love theme may evoke repudiation from nuns and spinsters and breed boredom in the minds of general readers, but like Sappho in Greek Literature, like Elizabeth Barret Browning in English letters, and like Anne Sexton and Sylvia Plath in modern American poetry, Mrs. Das offers us a feast of vivid images of love couched in felicitous language. No doubt, love is her 'forte' in poetry."[3]

But for Kamala Das love is not an end in itself; the culmination of it is the achievement of a meaning for life that is not to be found in the present modes and modalities of living. Since the genesis of love is our being in the world, her concept of love does not reject the seat of it, that is the body. She favours expression of love in its fullest measure in the interpersonal relationships. This belief in the reciprocity of the physical and the metaphysical aspects of love is clearly expressed in her poem 'The Suicide' wherein she says :

'Bereft of soul
My body shall be bare

Bereft of body
My soul shall be bare'

('The Suicide' — *The Descendants*)

Love, for her, is an invitation between two personalities with an intention to measure the mutual depths of each other. Not that the depth is measurable; but then, the whole world is made of an intention. So, Kamala Das makes her poetry a profound poetic expression of an intention only. What she violently pleads for is a possible understanding between men and women as equanimously independent personalities in an atmosphere of what the Christian fathers call 'agape.' But for the poet, her ideal lover is nowhere to be found. On Kamala Das's search for such a lover, Sunanda P. Chavan rightly observes :

> "Kamala Das's search for ideal love and the resultant disappointment seem to involve the psychological phenomenon of 'the animus' struggling to project the masculine imprint as interpreted by Jung. The attempt to seek in every lover, the perfection of masculine being is destined to end in failure because of the impossibility of realizing the ideal in human form."[4]

'In 'An Introduction' the poet speaks about her first bitter experience of getting rejected in love, which was enough to shatter all her adolescent dreams :

'When I asked for love, not knowing what else to ask
For, he drew a youth of sixteen into the
Bedroom and closed the door
He did not beat me
But my sad woman body felt beaten
The weight of my breasts and womb crushed me.

('An Introduction')

Thus, man's indifference to woman's pursuit of perfect being becomes a major pre-occupation in her poetry. This incompatibility is the source of frustration in the poet, and she asks :

'Can't this man with
Nimble finger tips unleash

Nothing more alive than the
Skin's lazy hungers?

('The Freaks,' *Summer In Calcutta*)

The man's indifference towards her longings is counteracted by that of hers towards the physical act of sex :

'It's only
To save my face, I flaunt, at
Times, a grand, flamboyant lust.'

('The Freaks')

In her poem 'The Old Playhouse' she repeats about this failure on the part of the man to respond to her love :

'It was not to gather knowledge
Of yet another man that I came to you but to learn
What I was, and by learning, to learn to grow but every
Lesson you gave was about yourself. You were pleased
With my body's response, its weather, its usual shallow
Convulsions.'

('The Old Playhouse,' *The old Playhouse and Other Poems*)

And again in 'In Love,'
'and his limbs like pale and
Carnivorous plants reaching
Out for me, and the sad lie
Of my unending lust'

('In Love,' *Summer In Calcutta*)

Love is an authentic phenomenon both conceptual and perceptual simultaneously. In the conceptual context it is Platonic and a chimera. In the perceptual context it dwindles into what can be called the creaturely evocative dimension. There is no possibility of reconciling both. They both are simultaneously felt experiences, hence, the love-hate tangle towards the very prospect of love in life. The essential dilemma in Kamala Das's poetry emerges out of this simultaneous predominance of love in its highest and lowest dimensions, that puts her on verbal excruciations flaring into abject ravings of a thoughtless creature wriggling under the ideological pressures of life. So her felt existential condition is like that of the cocroach of Kafka's 'Metamorphosis.' Hence, life as given for Kamala Das is a Kafkaish unending agony through a trial.

Towards the end, 'An Introduction' acquires a change in tone; the personal details begin to dissipate and give way to the universal :

'I met a man, loved him. Call
Him not by any name, he is every man
Who wants a woman, just I am every
Woman who seeks love.'

('An Introduction')

The expressions 'wants' and 'seeks' are allusions to man's superficial attitude towards love which is probably in contrast to woman's search for totality and permanence. The categorical distinction and differentiation between man and woman as naturalistic creatures puts man as a self-serving conservative agent, serving his own purposes, and cold-shouldering his feminine counterpart into a state of negligence and unwantedness. Against woman's total submission of her mind and body to man, he

'is tightly packed like the
Sword in his sheath.'

('An Introduction')

On a close scrutiny of the ways of Nature, it appears that it never had a programme of ultimate happiness or the highest pleasure for beings by way of sexual or spiritual fulfilment in the context of male-female union. This absence of the sublime in the life of the creatures is due to the incompatibility of the masculine and feminine entities. This fact is beautifully expressed in the following lines :

'In him the hungry haste
Of rivers'

('An Introduction')

that has the principal suggestion at the thoughtless urgency of man in being an aggressive partner, and

'in me the ocean' tireless
Waiting'

('An Introduction')

where the 'ocean' metaphor speaks for the profound manner in which the female partner patiently awaits the arrival of the 'river.'

The awareness of the impending defeat at the end in the pursuit of consummate love, makes the battle all the more difficult to comprehend. This failure in reaching the summit makes the human existence not greater than that of any other creature on earth. This creaturely approach enables Kamala Das to observe the self more objectively. This is 'the mind that sees and hears and/Is aware,' which is rather a curse than a relief to her sensitive consciousness. In this context Devendra Kohli's remarks about 'An Introduction' are worth quoting :

> "It is a part of the strength of Kamala Das's exploration of love-theme that it also follows her compulsions to articulate and understand the workings of the feminine consciousness. Her best known poem in this category, 'An Introduction' is concerned with the question of human identity."[5] and "is perhaps at the heart of any attempt at self-exploration and self-integration."[6]

'An Introduction' culminates in a note of failure, disappointment and reconciliation :

> 'Who are you, I ask each and every one,
> The answer is, it is I. Anywhere and
> Everywhere, I see the one who calls himself
> I.................
> It is I who drink lonely
> Drinks at twelve midnight, in hotels of strange towns,
> It is I who laugh, it is I who make love
> And then feel shame, it is I, dying
> With a rattle in my throat.
> I am sinner, I am saint.
> I am the beloved and the
> Betrayed. I have no joys which are not yours, no
> Aches which are not yours. I too call myself I.'

'An Introduction' can well be viewed as a poetic summation of the post-menstrual forebodings of a girl just being introduced into the world of the grown-ups where a pre-determined role awaits her. It is the experience of any girl entering her pubescence, descending from her private domain of colourful adolescent dreams to a world of many social and familial dictates.

These anxieties at first lead to fear and then to anger, but finally they lead her to a realization of the vanity of human existence, and a resultant reconciliation.

'An Introduction,' thus, makes the graphic touch-and-go of almost all the major thematic concerns dealt with in the whole poetic property of Kamala Das. The personal beginnings (exposition), the fear and fury (consummation) and the ultimate realization (a helpless reconciliation), combined with a conversational style, lend 'An Introduction' the overtones of a dramatic lyric. The poem rises above the initial gender concerns, and acquires aesthetic heights through the universality of its vision, its poignant realization of the pathetic nature of human imperfection and creatureliness. The autobiographical formula adopted for the poem gives it an immense authenticity and openness.

REFERENCES

1. Das, Kamala. "My Instinct, My Guru" *Indian Literature,* Vol. 31, No. 1 (Jan.-Feb. 1988) : 161.
2. Nabar, Vrinda. *The Endless Female Hungers : A Study of Kamala Das* (New Delhi : Sterling Publishers Pvt. Ltd., 1994) : 31.
3. Dwivedi, A.N. "As a Poet of Love and Sex," *Kamala Das And Her Poetry* (Delhi : Doaba House, 1983) : 32.
4. Chavan, Sunanda P. "As Moderns II : Kamala Das." *The Fair Voice : A Study of Indian Women Poets in English* (New Delhi : Sterling Publishers Pvt. Ltd., 1984) : 64.
5. Kohli, Devendra. "Kamala Das," *Contemporary Indian English Verse : An Evaluation*, Chirantan Kulshrestra (Ed.) (New Delhi : Arnold Heinemann, 1980) : 188.
6. Devendra.

7

Kamala Das : Homeless in the City

Z.F. MOLVI*

Kamala Das gained recognition as a poetess of considerable talent in the sixties with the publication of her collection *Summer in Calcutta* (1965). It was her outspoken and bold idiom that attracted the attention of the readers initially. However, her subsequent volumes such as *The Descendants* (1967) and *The Old Play House and Other Poems* (1973) have enlarged the thematic range of Indian English Poetry, bringing within its ambit, the hitherto unexplored areas of personal conflicts and power relations in the society. In examining the nature of urban experience in her poetry, the focus will be on how it defines her choice of themes and dictates her stylistic strategies. A.N. Dwivedi in his study of her poetry observes :

> Mrs. Das is a poet no so much of the countryside as of the city... . The city is an integral part of her existence and she can't shake off its impressions and memories easily.[1]

She has lived for long stretches of time in such metropolitan cities as Calcutta, Bombay, Delhi and Colombo. Her autobiography, *My Story*, contains descriptions of some of these cities and the kind of life she lived there.

It was her shift from the sheltered life of the village to the fast-paced, mechanical life of the city that sparked off her poetic

***Lecturer, Department of English, Navjivan Arts and Science College, Gujarat University, Dahod.**

utterances. The emotional centre of her early poems revolves around the shock she received at the sudden exposure to the city life. She spent her childhood and early stage of adolescence in the City of Calcutta where her father occupied a managerial post in a British Company. Her impressions of Calcutta may be gathered from her first collection, *Summer in Calcutta* (1965). The title poem of this first collection evokes an anxious passionate state of mind where memory and desire mingle.

It is also a moment of warm intoxication when sensuousness obliterates the worries of existence :

> Dear, forgive
> This moment's lull in
> wanting you, the blur.
> In memory. How Brief
> the term of my Devotion,
> how brief Your reign when
> I with Glass in hand, drink,
> drink, And drink again this
> Juice of April suns.

(*The Old Playhouse and Other Poems*, p. 24)

The search for a moment of ecstasy and oblivion is reflected in these words. But, beneath the surface sensuousness, is the nagging discontent of unfulfilled desires. In *My Story* she writes :

> There were at least a dozen men deeply infatuated with me. And yet I feared Calcutta. I longed to escape from it.[2]

So she was deeply torn between the desire to plunge into the materialistic pleasures of the city and an impulse to escape from its gross and degenerate vulgarities. This conflict was to become a focal theme in her later poetry. According to Bruce King,

> the contrast between a familiar, secure, loving home and the world she now experiences since leaving her family for marriage, its dissatisfactions and love affairs is the theme of 'The Corridores.'[3]

"Why do I so often dream
Of a house where each silent

Corridor leads me to warm
Yellow rooms — and, loud voices
Welcome me, and rich, friendly
Laughter, and upturned faces.
.... once awake, I
See the bed from which my love
Has fled, the empty room, the
Naked walls, count on fingers
My very few friends."

(*The Old Playhouse and Other Poems*, p. 45)

The poem 'An Apology to Gautama' brings out clearly the nature of the conflict stated in 'Summer in Calcutta.' Here she contrasts her lover and Gautama and highlights the difference between the ascetic and the sensual.

The opposition is between two modes of apprehending the world, the two ways of seeing :

.... while your arm hold
My woman — form, his hurting arms
Hold my very soul.

('An Apology to Gautama,'
Summer in Calcutta)

Here Gautama stands for a metaphysical mode of knowing the essence while her lover has access only to her body. As a woman poet, Kamala Das was quick to notice that the materialistic culture of the city concealed a spiritual void. She could indulge in the physical pleasures of the city only if she turned a blind eye to the metaphysical urges of the artist in her. As time passed, she noticed that the same spiritual blindness also gave rise to other prejudices. The city values only appearances and spectacles. It has no use for delicate feelings or finer sentiments. As a woman she valued her bonds with nature, family and the people in her immediate surroundings.

As an artist she attached significance to a humanistic attitude to the problems of existence.

However, the city constantly reduced her to a sexual object.

A.N. Dwivedi has rightly remarked,

"As a poet of the city, Kamla Das constantly employs the metaphor of the city for life such as in the poem 'A New City.'"[4]

I have come with only a picnic bag
To this new city
To seek a blind date, toshed as snakes do,
In coils and coils, my
Weariness.

('A New City,' *Summer in Calcutta*, p. 38)

There is an anguished awareness on the part of the poetess of having lost something in adopting the city as her home but she is also aware of the joys and amenities to be found in a city. Bruce King observes :

While marriage has hurt her ego, leaving her unfulfilled, her poems also record a woman enjoying the newness of the world as she wanders the streets and pursues her own interest.[5]

In her autobiography she comments :

all the Delhi streets were fragrant and murky. I felt very young, very lovely and delightfully carefree.

(*My Story*, p. 144)

Elsewhere she contrasts the inviolable peace of the Delhi landscape with her disturbed mind. She bids a touching farewell to the city of her long residence, Bombay, which she loves deeply :

I take leave of you, fair city, while tears
Hide somewhere in my adult eyes
And sadness is silent as a stone
In the river's unmoving
Core ......
It's goodbye, goodbye, goodbye,
To slender shapes behind windowpanes
Shut against indiscriminate desire
And rain.....

("Farewell to Bombay," *Summer in Calcutta*, p. 39)

The departure is as painful as the parting of a loved one, as the city forms an integral part of the emotional make up of the poet. In her analysis of Kamala Das's poems, K. Radha comments :

> In 'Farewell to Bombay' she is grieved at the prospect of leaving 'the fair city' the city where slender shapes peer behind closed window panes, where flesh-hungry birds circle in the sky with shrill and hostile cries, and where crowds gather near the sea, talking endlessly.[6]

'Of Calcutta' is a lengthy poem written in the form of a monologue addressed to the city of Calcutta and it is full of recollections. We notice that the city of Calcutta is depicted as the setting against which her emotional development is charted.

After thirty years the city has greatly changed. Every recollection is presented in the context of the city of Calcutta. Kamala Das recollects her love affair in her childhood as well as her love for the city which nurtured her love like a mother. Therefore she says,

> .... yes, our Calcutta,
> where we loved as children once, both you
> And I, our eyes, dark nests where daydreams roosted,[7]
>
> ('Of Calcutta,' *CP*, Vol. 1, p. 56)

As the poem proceeds further, we come across many references to certain places in Calcutta beginning with the school itself, its French window, the wall-clock, the ayah of the hostel, loneliness of the playground and the pink-walled chamber. She remembers the particular place where she used to meet her lover, also the Rickshaw pullers and the game of badminton. Her friend Rama Sahgal lived in the red house at Ballygunge Circular Road. There are references to her Austrian teacher and the noisy Harish Mukharji Road.

There is a shift when Kamala Das begins to reflect on her later life particularly in the following lines :

> Years have sped along and I stand before you like
> The wreck of your dreams, the sad debris of a storm,
> Breasts sagging, hair greying and the fine lines forming,
> Beneath my eyes ? Unwisely we had left our home
> The only mother-city in the world and not

Meeting once, not even at the Woodburn Park's
Morning tennis, allowed to children then, or at

('Of Calcutta,' *CP.*, Vol. 1, p. 58)

Thus, Calcutta is a mother-city for her as she was brought up tenderly in the lap of it. There is conflict between the childhood's city which is distant now and the present state of unfulfilled desires and nostalgia. Thus, the city life has fragmented and disintegrated herself which is evident in the following lines :

Here in my husband's home, I am a trained circus dog
Jumping my routine hoops each day, where is my soul,
My spirit, where the muted tongues of my desire?
Our childhood's city is distant now..........

'(Of Calcutta,' *CP*, Vol. 1, p. 59)

Kamala Das yearns for the same city where she had passed her childhood, for the city also undergoes certain changes with the course of time. The city of her childhood is as much beyond her reach as her own childhood. What she learns from this encounter with the city is her essential homelessness. She says :

Here we shall be always a little bit lost, this cannot
be our home.

Thus, the urban experience terminates in her awareness about her own homeless state.

This poem reminds us of Pritish Nandy's poem 'Calcutta. If You Must Exile Me' in which he describes the Squalor and slums of Calcutta very vividly. He loves the city so deeply that he appeals to the city poignantly in this way.

Calcutta if you must exile me, wound my lips
before I go

Calcutta if you must exile me burn my eyes
before I go.

And finally

Calcutta if you must exile me destroy my sanity
before I go.[8]

We do not find such sentimental attachment to the city in the poem, 'Of Calcutta.' Calcutta signifies a period of innocence in her own personal past, and the city is associated with beautiful unforgettable romantic experience.

Kamala Das' first collection 'Summer in Calcutta' was published in 1965. It contains only fifty poems. This work opens with the poem 'The Dance of the Eunuchs' which sets the ironical tone that continues to dominate the other two volumes, *The Descendants* (1967) and *The Old Playhouse and Other Poems* (1973).

Dancing eunuchs are a familiar sight in several Indian cities. The poem begins with the description of the hot weather which makes the dance of the eunuchs more pitiable. The word 'hot' is repeated. Also, the repetition of the nasal sound through the words 'clashing and jingling' produces a musical effect which evokes the movement of dance. As the poem proceeds, their whirling movement and extended frenzy are contrasted with an inner vaccuity and so these movements become mere convulsions. Kamala Das describes in graphic images their sterile world of vacant ecstasy where their voices are harsh, their bodies are like half burnt legs from funeral pyres. Besides, their songs are melancholic as they sang of dying lovers and of unborn children. At the end of the poem they are called poor creatures because even crows and children are not delighted at their dance. They remain silent spectators. The rainfall is also not sufficient to bring coolness. Thus, the poet has expressed sympathy for eunuchs who are exiled from the normal world of human relations and suffer a peculiar irony of fate. A.N. Dwivedi has rightly pointed out :

> The poem is powerful and bold indeed and displays an admirable sense of proportion in the use of imagery and metaphor.[9]

She spent part of her childhood in Calcutta but she was born in Malabar and her consciousness is deeply rooted in her native soil. The poetry becomes more accessible in the light of her autobiography *My Story*.

If one wants to read her poetry directly, it is better to begin with her poems 'An Introduction' and 'A Faded Epaulet on His Shoulder' (p. 103). Both the poems reveal much information about her political knowledge, creative talent, bitter experiences in married life, her illicit love affairs, frustration and loneliness, and above all her quest for identity, an attempt for self-exploration and self-integration.

When she moved to the city she left behind in her village a loving grandmother and a crumbling ancestral house of haunting memories. As a critic observes :

> She has come to associate lust and loss of love with the repulsive aspects of urban experiences.[10]

There are several poems which illustrate that she regrets her moving away from the sight and sounds of idyllic country-side surrounding her pastoral house to the dusty cities with their din and disturbance. Like Nissim Ezekiel, she depicts the squalor and the heat, the crowd and the slum of city life but her presentation is different because her irony is not bitter and she is not completely alienated from social milieu.

It seems that her womanhood is unbearable and painful to her. As she tells us in the poem 'An Introduction' she wore a shirt and her brother's trousers, cut her hair and ignored her womanliness.

But in the highly urbanized society she is advised by categorizers to conform to its rules :

> My womanliness. Dress in sarees, be girl
> Be wife, they said. Be embroiderer, be cook,
> Be a quarreller with servants. Fit in. Oh,
> Belong, cried the categorizers

('An Introduction,'
The Old Playhouse and Other Poems, p. 27)

She does obey this advice and wears different masks in the male-dominated urban society but she fails miserably. If at all she gains or achieves something through these different roles, it is a sort of self-realization about the paradoxical nature of herself but it comes through empathy and the poem ends with the painful assertion,

> I am saint. I am the beloved and the
> Betrayed, I have no joys which are not yours,
> no Aches which are not yours. I too call
> myself I.

('An Introduction,'
The Old Playhouse and Other Poems, p. 27)

Yet one feels that this painful assertion is not philosophical or theological answering the basic question 'who am I'? It is an existential solution that she opts for. The theme of the above poem is her anguish and suffering. Some of the recurring themes of confessional poetry may be traced in this attitude towards experience. As a critic points out :

> The painful assertion, "I too call myself I" comes from the predicament of the confessional poet. Her experiences are common and ordinary in fact too common to give her any special identity. But the "I" which experiences them, she insists, is separate and unique. This, to her, is the only way to retain her sense of personal worth in the world of categorizers. She sees the outer world as hostile to the world of the self.[11]

We come to know about her private or personal life through her book *My Story*. Kamala Das was married at the early age of fifteen and at the age of nineteen she had a nervous breakdown as she found herself a neglected wife. She was almost confined to a room which made her seriously ill and subsequently she was taken to Malabar where her affectionate grandmother could cure her. She has been very much attached to her grandmother. Her grandmother was deeply attached to her old ancestral house. The poem 'My Grandmother's House' begins with the lines :

> There is a house now far away where once
> I received love. That woman died,

('My Grandmother's House,' *CP*, Vol. 1, p. 120)

As the poem progresses, we feel her wistful nostalgia and at the end of the poem, she tells us that she was proud of that house because it gave her genuine love and true peace and comfort. Her present unsettled condition is contrasted with this scene of comfort. She has lost her right path and she has been reduced to a beggar seeking love at the stranger's house. Thus, the poem ends on a tragic note.

Even the description of the house is pathetic and she finds a great distance between the real but bitter world and the ideal world of her childhood, full of love.

Commenting on this poem, Anisur Rahman writes :

> Kamala Das identified her grandmother, with the old house, which in turn, personifies human heart. Irony plays a vital role in her poetry emerging as a dominant poetic strategy.[12]

But one feels that this poetic strategy is natural to her and she does not appear to apply it as a conscious act of craftsmanship. Her desire to go to her old grandmother's house becomes more intense when she thinks of her own house or compares it with her husband's house which is evident in the poem 'The Old Playhouse.' The poem is addressed to her husband and it begins with irony and pathos. The images of swallow and flight are appropriately used to express feminine experience particularly as a wife. As the poem proceeds further, its emotional effect is intensified with the repetition of the address 'You' which is charged with poignancy and the line 'You called me wife,' is highly ironical which stands in sharp contrast to its beginning.

> You planned to tame a swallow, to hold her
> In the long summer of your love so that
> she would forget

('The Old Playhouse,'
The Old Playhouse and Other Poems, p. 1)

The poem begins with a mild satirical tone. Her nature is exposed to us and we feel that she likes freedom most but she finds herself in the cage like a bird. Her urge to fly and her pre-occupation with self is reduced gradually for she becomes the victim of male lust which is expressed in the following lines :

> You dribbled spittle into my mouth, you poured
> Yourself into every nook and cranny, you embalmed
> My poor lust with your hitter-sweet juices.

('The Old Playhouse,'
The Old Playhouse and Other Poems, p. 1)

This shows her disgust at such kind of male treatment. Then Kamala Das uses the images of saccharine, vitamins, artificial light, air-conditioner, out-flower in the vases in order to represent mechanical or monotonous and hypocritical, modern urban society which has usurped her will and reason, as well as her singing and dance. Therefore, her mind is an old playhouse without any light. She always seeks true and pure love which she does not receive and she represses her anger in this way.

> The strong man's technique is
> Always the same, he serves his love is lethal doses,
>
> ('The Old Playhouse,'
> *The Old Play-house and Other Poems*, p. 1)

Her counterpart knows the technique of making her submissive but love to her is a way of learning about one's own self. She comes to him for she wanted to realize her true self. Instead she loses her freedom and is reduced to a prisoner by his egotism. She loses her natural mirth, thus, she is not able to forget the scars of the male lust on her body.

It is possible to trace a deepening sense of crisis in Kamala Das's relation with the city. As was pointed out above, the break with the world of innocence coincided with her marriage and shift to the cosmopolitan chaos of Bombay. Coming as it does at the onset of adolescence the city becomes the venue of her first major crisis in life.

The denial of love and the need to put on the mask of an obedient housewife add to this crises. At this stage she becomes aware of the subtle power relations that inform life and the city. Bruce King comments :

> Alongside Das's unfulfilled need for love, another prominent subject of her poems is the need to assert, to conquer, to dominate.[13]

The hierarchical power structure of the city is masculine in its authoritatrian disregard for human sentiments. The phrase 'the strong man's technique' shows her awareness about the repressive nature of the male authority. The materialistic world of the city is equally repressive. It does not let the individual to exist as a dignified human being. In a large number of poems she speaks about the brutalising aspects of the urban experience. The predatory elements predominate all its dealings.

The poem 'After the Party' is an apt illustration of this predatory nature of the city. We notice that she expresses her different moods which are mostly depressing and disappointing. Her experience is basically shaped by urban life as can be seen in 'White Man with Whiter Legs.' The opening lines say :

> We learn from our surroundings as animals do or birds for
> Our copyings we are not to be blamed. Our city crushes
> Its inhabitants one by one and with urban finesse eats
> Them, and afterwards sits facing the moon picking its
> teeth while
> The fetor of its breath fills our mottled lungs at night.
>
> ('White Man with Whiter Legs,'
> *CP*, Vol. II, p. 86)

The poem is reflective and at the end of the poem she acknowledges the powerful influence of the body over her quest for true love. The city begets only slayers. As she says :

> Each mother suckles her own enemy
> And hate is first nurtured at her gentle breast
> and each man's seed
> Is pregnant with his death.
>
> ('White Man with Whiter Legs,'
> *CP*, Vol. I, p. 86)

This statement as applied to the society in general can be interpreted as a comment on the corrupting nature of the urban experience. The city crushes as well as corrupts its inhabitants. The masculine authority of the city manifests itself in its corrupting influence which turns its inhabitants into victims.

In 'The House Builders' Kamala Das shows how amidst the squalor of the city the migrant labourers make a desperate effort to hold on to life in their collective effort. The poetess sympathizes with the houseless workers who are engaged in 'building houses for the alien rich.' The poem is built upon a contrast between the alien rich and the working class people. Throughout the poem she uses nature images to describe these people. These men concave like the cicades in brambled foliage. They occasionally listen to the joyful film songs but the dream-world of the cinema is far away from the harsh reality they live. As they sing these merry tunes their voices break. There is nothing in their life which is comparable to the hero's happiness. It is too big a lie for their throats to swallow.

This part of the poem brings out the sharp contrast between the dream worlds the modern commercial city sells people and the misery of their daily routine.

Though these people are uprooted and without a shelter they are not totally homeless, because homelessness is a state of total alienation from the living world around us. Though they are exploited, they are not brutalised to the extent of being dehumanised. The poet refers to their robust lust, ribald sounds and native grace. Their hands which are like the withered boughs of some mystic hodoo tree cast only cool shadows. 'Withered' suggests exploitation but 'cool shadows' is a pointer to the humanity they retain. With natural grace they bestow vast shelters even on unbelievers. These unbelievers are the alien rich for whom these unfortunate people are building houses.

The poem shows the basic dialectic operating in Kamala Das's poetry. She finds that even in the midst of the city's misery these people are able to sustain their humanity. In Kamala Das's poetry city often stands for exploitation, dehumanisation, corruption, brutalisation and homelessness. But human beings who can reach out to others and communicate with them can successfully overcome some of these violent impacts of the city.

In the city, Kamala Das encounters the predatory element of the human beings in their menacing aspects. In 'After the Party' she describes men as dark and sleek like drones.

Obviously they are idlers who do not work to earn their bread. The women are parakeets suggesting their vulnerability. The images of blood and violence suggested by 'The River Veins' make the party a scene of wild encounters. The male glance is full of lust and she is defenceless against such open displays of male authority. In Kamala Das's poetry the city is the centre of masculine authority. The woman or the working class people are unable to survive as human beings in such surroundings. She enters the party as a celibate by choice. This means that she does not want to be drawn into the game which is a trap laid by the powerful male. When she leaves the party she sees the fullness of her body in the lift mirror.

It is tamed by will and practice and has been taught never to make demands. It takes all her will power and alertness to escape unscathed from the party. This encounter brings out the risks a woman is exposed to in the urban milieu. Just as 'The House Builders' describes the brutal misery of the houseless working class people, the poem 'After the Party' describes the tragic solitude of the woman who refuses to be a sexual object.

In the poem 'Honour' Kamala Das lays bare the hollowness of the upper class claims to honour. Her own problem is that she belongs to the middle class but she is aware of the hypocrisy of her class. When the Dalit Panther group, an association of the depressed class people, came to seek her blessings she knew she could tell him nothing that was not hypocrisy. Her silence was seen as an endorsement of their ideological stand.

She had long been accustomed to the double standards the society adopted in dealing with the honour of people. In the feudal set up of her village in Kerala, she had seen women being cruelly discarded or even killed after subjecting them to gross misuse. She knows that the lower class people in the city share a similar fate of being hunted down by the powerful. It is in this perception of power relations that inform the urban society that Kamala Das differs from other Indian English poets.

In several poems, Kamala Das refers to her confinement in the hospital for various illnesses. The world of the hospital is a metaphor for the modern world which is sick and sickening and also for the body. Bruce King sees a basic dualism in her writing in which soul is contrasted to body. He comments that

> she seems to imagine overcoming this dualism only through death.[14]

It is her sense of vulnerability occasioned by the insecurity she feels in the city that makes her think about her body. Her womanhood becomes a curse and illness is a way of escape. When she talks about the inmates of the lunatic asylum, she says that they were brave enough to escape to step out of 'the brute regimental of same routine.' The city is a place where the same routine is worshipped. The old or the sick have no place in the scheme of the city. The marginalisation of such classes is poignantly portrayed in the poem

'Old Cattle.' When the poetess is being taken home after being in the city nursing home for three weeks she notices some old cattle being driven to the slaughter-house near the mountain passes.

Even as they moved towards their death, they paused to chew at the shrubs for a moment. The poet felt like joining them because in her sick condition she was no better than them. In the materialistic environment of the city only those who contribute towards its wealth have the right to survive. This blindness of the city becomes the central theme in many of her poems.

The poet uses the word 'homeless' in 'Floatsam' for those who drift in life without a definite goal or purpose. The sexual act gives a temporary sense of home because it saves them from loneliness. She feels that the kind of solitude she suffers turns her house into a desert. It is pertinent to see the larger implications of this sense of homelessness. Bruce King has observed :

> Her poems are situated neither in the act of sex nor in feelings of love: they are instead involved with the self and its varied, often conflicting emotions, ranging from the desire for Security and intimacy to the assertion of the ego, self-dramatization and feelings of shame and depression.[15]

Her poems examine the basic dilemmas of a mind which cannot feel at home in the city. Her search for love is part of a larger quest for motherhood and home which cannot be understood by the commercialized urban sensibility. When she is denied every channel of self-realization as a woman and as an individual, she feels hunted and persecuted. The urban experience in Kamala Das constitutes this scene of conflict and anguish.

In the poetry of Kamala Das, the world of harmony and love is symbolised by her grandmother. With her grandmother's death she woke upto the brutal facts of life. That this period also coincided with her entrance into adolescence complicates her transformation to a woman. The earlier order of innocence and love gave way to the adult world of lust and hypocrisy. In the poem 'The Millionaires at Marine Drive' she says that her grandmother was buried in the loose red soil of her heart. Ever since that death she has searched in vain for true love. Those who flocked around her came to rob her of youth. Instead of love, they only knew the language of lust. Only after losing her youth, she could come out of this world of lust and greed. She sees the millionaires of Bombay scattering grain to the doves early in the morning. She sees a pain in the fluttering of their wings. Obviously the city knows no real love. It reduces everyone who seeks love to a beggar. The dove is an image of the innocent woman. The fluttering of their wings was laughter, crazed with pain. The millionaires are obviously proud of their generosity but lacks the sensitivity to see the act of charity reducing free birds to bonded creatures. In the last part of the poem, she comments on her present stage of deprivation. She knows that her life lacks meaningful content. The show goes on since she has to carry on in her role as a respectable housewife but she knows that behind her painted mask, there is a fog of hate. She concludes with a comforting thought that somewhere lovers must still be communicating with each other but she has turned old, frigid and grey haired. There is nothing that she can look forward to.

Kamala Das's rebellion against the masks of the city has to be understood against the positive values she attaches to the experience of love. Though the concluding lines of this poem may appear sentimental, they are a tribute to the humanising tenderness of love that nurtures a sublime state of mind akin to spirituality. Beside the gross degenerate brutalising traits of urban life such a romantic dream has its affirmative value. When the romantic dream looks totally out of place in the urban society she flaunts a bragging, unconventional self to register her protest. Her autobiography *My Story* is a narrative where this part of her rebellious personality is expressed. Since the city understands nothing but the sensational language, she transforms herself into a sensational event. In an article published in *Eve's Weekly* she pleads for "the return of a social order that allowed woman to have more than husband if she so desired."[16] In an article she wrote in *Debonair* titled 'I Have Lived Beautifully' she said :

> I often walked with young man along the sea
> flaunting my unconventionality.[17]

This attitude of defiance is expressed in some of her poems like 'The Freaks' where she says :

I am a freak.

In the poetry of Sylvia Plath too one comes across a similar theatrical posture, where an exhibitionist self is highlighted. This is a reaction to the fraudulent aspects of the city life. It is a self-preservative act to save oneself from the corrupt influence of the city. She says in 'Loud Posters' :

I have stretched my two dimensional
Nudity on sheets of weeklies, monthlies
Quarterlies, a sad sacrifice.

(*The Old Playhouse and Other Poems*, p. 47)

The poetry of Kamala Das is marked by mercurial changes of mood, attitude and tone. From a mood of celebration and affirmation she can swing to one of morbid depression in a few lines. In 'Luninol' she speaks of guarding an inner space of the soul (the soul's 'mute arena') where the ruthless one cannot enter. If the theatrical posture struck by an exhibitionist self is one way of preserving the self, resorting to the use of sleeping pills to reach 'that silent sleep inside your sleep' is a similar act of defending the self. These extremes of swinging moods reflect the complexity of the urban experience treated in her poems.

Her womanhood complicates her perception of urban experience as we can see in poems like 'Ferns' and 'Gino.' In the poem 'Ferns' we come across images of candle, ferns, shores and mountains. She has used metaphors in order to express her powerful emotions. For instance,

The pale street's horror, and run with the wind

(Line 6)

When words, while uttered, will fall thudding down
Like dismembered heads and love will ride damp

(Lines 12, 13)

Shores and mountains where darkness grows like ferns

('Ferns,' *CP*, Vol. 1, p. 43)

The central image here is that of 'fern' which is a type of green plant with featherly shaped leaves and no flowers.

Thus, she has described her love budding like ferns but in vain. She sees her femininity as a kind of sterile bondage.

Her poem 'Gino' reveals the terror of sex in the very opening lines :

> You will perish from his kiss, he said, as one must
> Surely die, when bitten by a krait who fills
> The bloodstream with its accursed essence.

('Gino,' *CP*, Vol. l, p. 83)

She expresses a sense of disgust at male habits and treatment as noticed in the poem 'The Old House.' The lover's kiss is compared with a krait's bite in order to express the horror of sex. The lover is like a reptile who keeps on sucking the female body. Love as it is manifested in her life causes a sense of death, thus, one feels that it is very difficult to draw the demarcation line between life and death as well as love and lust. There is a desire to experience true love but it turns poisonous even outside marriage. Kamala Das has expressed her views on adultery frankly in her book *My Story*. She has said that she found it distasteful and she hated the exploitations of her body. She confesses that it ruins the beautiful relationship between individuals. Thus, we find a kind of conflict between her ideal desire and the actual or real experience both in her married life and in her private affairs outside the marriage. Besides, it seems difficult to overcome this conflict which is evident in these lines :

> If I could only dislodge the inherited
> Memory of a touch,

('Gino,' *CP*, Vol. l, p. 83)

Neither can she give up her ideal desire nor can she forget her sexual experience. Obviously, happiness for her is a remote possibility and she finally ends up losing both self and freedom. The impersonal setting of hospitals and lunatic asylums deepens her anxious state of mind. She dreams of sepulchral ward-boys wheeling her through long corridors to the X-ray room's dark interior, 'the clatter of the trolleys with the dead on them.' What is frightening about the hospitals and clinics is their commercial attitude towards human suffering.

In the next section she contrasts the dream world of desire with the real world of sickness and old age. She wears her body without joy. It is owned by her lover, 'man of substance' and it has no defence against his impersonal lust. In her struggle against this loss of face she imagines the common fate that awaits her. She will probably end up being the fatkneed hag in the long bus queue 'from whose shopping bag the mean potato' must roll across the road. The use of the word 'mean' suggests the banality of her common life and her fear of being reduced to an object of ridicule. She also envisages herself as the patient on the hospital bed 'lying in drugged slumber and dreaming of home.' This is the state of being confined to a prison-like place. However, a change of mood comes with the line, 'I shall be the grandmother willing away her belongings.' But even here the scraps and trinkets lasting than her bones. It is the oppressive sense of death that envelops her here completely.

Devendra Kohli has rightly asserted :

> The cumulative burden of domesticity, routine sickness and the anticipation of death are sensitively portrayed (in this poem) that the final passage must be quoted in full especially because the word 'convulse' with its clinical associations reminds us of the 'Convulsions' of the eunuchs in the first poem in 'Summer in Calcutta.'[18]

In the last four lines she evokes a sense of annihilation because the poem which begins with a reference to death ends with these words :

> perhaps some womb in that
> Darker world shall convulse, when I finally enter,
> A legitimate entrant, marked by discontent

('Gino,' *CP*, Vol. l, p. 85)

The womb of death does not hold any promise of a renewal. Marked by discontent, she will be a victim of the dark forces of evil. Commenting on the technique of the poem Anisur Rahman has remarked :

> Her method is to begin from the personal and travel identifiable regions beyond the ego. The process of selection and rejection is her vital means and remains a constant pre-occupation with her 'Gino' offers an apt illustration of this vital concern.[19]

When Kamala Das's discontent reaches its climax her thoughts turn suicidal. In the poem entitled 'Suicide' we listen to her painful utterance :

Bereft of soul
My body shall be bare
Bereft of body
My soul shall be bare.

('The Suicide,' *The Descendants*, p. 1)

The poem is addressed to the sea and it is presented in the form of a monologue.

The image of the sea has always been there in her consciousness right from her childhood when there was harmony between the soul and the body especially when she used to swim in a pale green-pond near her house in Malabar. As a critic points out in his article on Kamala Das, 'this harmony breaks away with the intervention of adulthood.' Here physical maturity is destructive and its suppression or even its fulfilment does not give her any mystical experience. This creates a kind of conflict between the world as it is and the personal experience. The poet cannot synthesize, the inner and the outer *i.e.* soul and the body as creator so she thinks of becoming her own negative creator by blowing up either of the two

O Sea, I am fed up
I want to be simple
I want to be loved
And
If I love is not to be had,
I want to be dead ...

('The Suicide,' *The Descendants*, p. 2)

Thus love is the essence of her life but in real life she has to wear the mask of a happy woman and wife in the male-dominated, urbanised Indian society. She has to maintain the distance between herself and the lower class people. She dislikes this. That is why she wants to be simple. There is a sense of nihilism in this poem. The image of the sea functions both as companion and killer. Her confession arouses pity and terror. Since her ideas are violent, the poem reveals her complex mental state. She has also used the image of an optical illusion for objectifying this state.

Even the powerful sun slumbers into the vortex of the sea. To her, the sea is a generous cow. Thus, the sea offers a kind of perennial shelter. The poem also reflects Indian sensibility where the river is always sacred for it gives life and it can become an agency of redemption. Kamala Das's idea of suicide emerges from her possessive nature. She fails miserably even to possess her own husband. The attempt to possess him engenders destructive tendencies :

It required drinks
To hold him down
To make him love.

('The Suicide,'
The Old Playhouse and Other Poems, p. 37)

Her failure is often due to her double consciousness which leads her to an awareness of the disintegration of her personality. In the innocent world of her childhood, she swam in the sea and in the guilty conscious world of her adulthood she swims in the body of her husband. This kind of escapes which she seeks in physical love are also attempts to efface oneself. At the end of the poem, she prefers soul because it is the soul that matters. It is the soul that knows how to sing even at the vortex of the sea. She requests the sea to take her naked soul which is more vital than her body.

Her encounters with the city finally force her to define herself in new terms. Her attempts at self-definition undergo several stages of change from the early 'Introduction' to the more recent poems. What is of interest to our present discussion is the fact that her feminine self finds itself at odds with the corrupt environment of the city. Her suicidal urge reflects her desperate desire to renew herself.

As can be seen in her several poems dealing with Radha and Krishna theme, the desire to transcend the limits set by the conventional society of the materialistic city is an essential element in her search for a new identity.

It will be instructive to discuss the poem 'Blood' in this context against the backdrop of her search for a new identity. The old house her grandmother lived in and her Nair heritage are referred to repeatedly in her poems. She often traces her blood to a royal lineage as her grandmother had told her during her childhood :

That we had the oldest blood,
My brother and she and I,
The oldest blood in the world,
A blood thin and clear and fine
While in the veins of the always poor
And in the veins
Of the new-rich ones

('Blood,' *CP*, Vol. 1, p. 4, 5)

As in the poem 'Honour' here also, the poet mocks at the fallacies of a feudal social order. She understands that the very idea of purity leads to prejudices which can complicate lives. But there is an emotional bond between her and her great grandmother. As Bruce King points out

> an inner core of identity to which she refers her name and aristocratic blood, her mother's family, life in the South and her youth in contrast to her marriage.[20]

It seems that Kamala Das is aware of the differences between the two classes the poor and the rich but she is always ironical whenever such feelings occur to her in an intensive form.

The poem begins with the narration of her childhood days with her brother and grandmother who is deeply attached to the old house. As the poem proceeds, Kamala Das portrays the picture of her house as well as relations of love. These memories are a source of authentic human feelings.

She gives the details of her grandmother's nature and her love for the decaying house. The poem is autobiographical and Kamala Das's nostalgia for the old house and for her grandmother is effectively reflected. There is no exaggeration in these emotions. Kamala Das is hurt on seeing the cracked and dilapidated house and the sight is as painful to her as the sight of the aged grandmother Therefore, she promises her,

When I grow old, I said,
And very very rich

I shall rebuild the fallen walls
And make new this ancient house

('Blood,' *CP*, Vol. 1, p. 4, 5)

But later in the poem we come across her honest confession and realization :

I had learnt by than
Most lessons of defeat
Had found out that to grow rich
Was a difficult feat

('Blood,' *CP*, Vol. 1, p. 5)

This realization only comes when one finds a great struggle in the city life where even the word 'struggle' is equated with life itself. A.N. Dwivedi remarks :

> More than the pathos of the memory of her grandmother the poem is concerned with the poet's sense of death and decay.[21]

He seems to overlook the fact that the poem also ends with the word 'Blood.' While what he says is valid it should be kept in mind that the poet remembers her ancestral house and village as a modern city-dweller. What the poem measures is the distance between her rural past and her urban present. The poetess does not wish her blood to be blamed at all for not fulfilling the promises given to her by her grand-mother although her blood has inherited and still carries that stately flavour.

Here her blood becomes an agency to recollect her glorious past and yet irony of fate that the same agency cannot bring desired changes. Perhaps it hints at feminine helplessness in the struggle against a male dominated world. The house is described twice in the poem, first from the grandmother's point of view and secondly from the poet's point of view. In the first, we find that the house becomes a symbol of decay and at the same time it arouses powerful feelings of attachment and love for it. Whereas in the second it causes a sense of death and becomes a symbol of irretrievable past, she would not mind being called callous or selfish but would never like to blame her blood. There is an element of self-pity in this acceptance of her inability to repair and reclaim the past while upholding its glorious heritage.

Kamala Das identifies with the sufferings of the mute victims of oppression. In 'House Builders' we have seen how she is concerned with the homeless workers who build houses for the alien rich. In 'Nani' she is haunted by the suicide of the pregnant maid who hanged herself in the privy while the poet was yet a child. To the children the hanging body turning gently on the rope as the wind blew appeared like a puppet doing a comic dance. After some years the poetess enquires of her grandmother about the dead maid. She pretends ignorance and the poetess remarks :

> With that question ended Nani. Each truth
> Ends thus with a query. It is this designed
> Deafness that turns mortality into
> Immortality, the definite into
> The soft indefinite.
>
> (*CP*, p. 18)

Embarrassing questions are ignored by us because we cannot face the truth. C.V. Venugopal remarks :

> The poetry of Kamala Das is full of questions that are rarely answered. They are queries about truth. But, truth, in general, is unbearable. And Kamala Das, the seeker after truth feels betrayed.

The wise ones live in a blue silent zone, 'unscratched by doubts.'[22]

Kamala Das has written a few poems based on her experiences in the city of Colombo. The ethnic strife exploded into a civil war between the Tamils and the Sinhalese while she was there. The city witnesses large scale violence against the Tamils. Poems like, 'The Sea of Galle Face Green,' 'Smoke in Colombo,' 'After July,' 'Shopper at Cornells, Colombo,' 'A Certain Defect in the Blood,' and 'Fear' deal with this face of urban violence. In 'The Sea at Galle Face Green' she says that the city of Colombo, once full of glory, has become a half burnt corpse. She describes the city under curfew in these words :

> The city was grey
> And every window was
> shut. Fear was in the air
> As the corpses smouldered,
> Fear and a stench sweets as

That of raw cashewnuts
Roastings. The sea did its
Duty as usual at
The Galle Face Green, without
A sign of fear, without
A sign of shock or pain
It patrolled the empty shore.

(*CP*, p. 13)

The sea appears indifferent to human suffering because it represents eternity whereas men are caught in time and history. In 'Smoke in Colombo' she describes the devastation of the city in the riots. Smoke lingered in the streets 'as grief lingers on within women rocking emptied craddles.' The image of the mother grieving for her dead child brings out the deep sense of anguish the poetess felt at the mindless violence that had reduced the city to rubble and smoke. In 'Shopper at the Cornells, Colombo' she tells us how she tried to conceal her Indianness while shopping.

'After July' and 'A Certain Defect in the Blood' are poems which boldly trace the ethnic conflict to the resurgence of fascist forces in the Sri Lankan society. Though Kamala Das is not a political poet in the conventional sense, as a victim of oppression, she is able to judge the nature of the crisis enveloping the society. After July there were no Tamils in sight in Colombo. No flower-seller came to the door with strings of Jasmine. Commenting on the aggressive display of brutal power which hunted down the Tamils she says :

Hitler rose from the dead, he demanded
Yet another round of applause, he hailed
The robust Aryan blood, the sinister
Brew that absolves a man of his sins and
Gives him the right to kill his former friends.

(*CP*, p. 15)

In 'A Certain Defect in the Blood' Kamala Das says that the elders could not answer the children's questions as to how the violence erupted between the two communities on the island. Their answer is far from being satisfactory :

It was a defect
In our blood that made us the land's inferiors,
A certain muddiness in the usual red,
Revealing our non-Aryan descent.

(*CP*, p. 17)

It is relevant to recall that in her early poems she had asserted her Dravidian identity. In the ethnic strife on the island, she finds intolerance of the majority community as a manifestation of the masculine display of power. In the plight of the persecuted minority she sees part of her own feminine self reflected. This is why she is able to identify with their displacement so deeply.

Commenting on Kamala Das's achievement as a poetess, Bruce King remarks :

> She brings a sense of locality to her poems. There are the rooms in which she lives, the homes she has left, the bedrooms, the restaurants and streets in which she meets her lovers, the rides in cars, the people she visits or notices, the people she addresses in personal terms. Whereas Ezekiel consciously refers to her environment, Das's poems assume their location, create their space by being set in situations rather than by observing or alluding to their environment.[23]

In Ezekiel's poetry the city is a permanent presence. It informs both his themes and style. Kamala Das on the other hand is an exile who finds the city hostile. She could never settle down and survive in the city like Ezekiel because she identifies the inner core of her identity with her rural childhood, grandmother's protective love and the nourishing bonds with the ancestral home. She finds the city as a male-dominated place where her feminine self cannot survive without wearing masks. She is asked to conform to the rules of the snobbish society. What is destructive to her feminine self is also detrimental to her art. While Ezekiel falls back on irony and distances himself from the crowd, Kamala Das identifies herself with the housebuilders who are homeless in the city though they build houses. She listens to the vacant ecstasy of the song of eunuchs who represent the void at the heart of the city. She rebels by consciously courting destruction or striking dramatic poses.

It is this difference in perception of the nature of the urban experience that explains the difference between the poetic styles of Kamala Das and Ezekiel. She is a bilingual writer who finds it necessary to express herself in two languages. In her famous poem 'An Introduction' she says that she speaks three languages, writes in two and dreams in one.

To those who advise her not to write in English because it is not her mother-tongue she replies that the language she speaks becomes hers, 'its distortions, its queerness.' It is half-English, half-Indian, funny perhaps, but it is honest. She says that is 'the speech of the mind that is here and not there, a mind that sees and hears and is aware.' Bruce King feels that Kamala Das's most remarkable achievement is writing in an Indian English :

> Often her vocabulary, idioms, choice of verbs, and some syntactical constructions are part of what has been termed the Indianization of English.[24]

The free verse of Kamala Das, thus, attempts to reflect her separate identity, her quest for love and her rejection of the corrupting influence of the city. Ezekiel in his 'Poet, Lover, Birdwatcher' says :

> The best poets wait for words :
> Kamala Das in 'Without a Pause' says :
> Write without
> A pause, don't search for pretty words
> Dilute the truth, but write in haste, of
> Everything perceived, and known and loved.

In 'Words' she says that words are a nuisance. Her poems are marked by a sense of urgency. In Ezekiel we feel that he chooses his words deliberately with an eye on the formal perfection of the poem. Kamala Das, on the other hand, trusts the emotional intensity of her experience to choose its own appropriate words. The anguish and rage we witness in Kamala Das is absent in Ezekiel. Kamala Das speaks as a displaced victim who cannot find shelter in the city. She associates city with the morbid, gloomy sides of her own experiences, though her healthy interest in people and places helps her to relate herself to the urban environment. Though she has lived most of her life in various large and small cities her poems depict her as an outsider in the city.

REFERENCES

1. A.N. Dwivedi. *Kamala Das And Her Poetry* (Delhi : Doaba House, 1983) : 25.
2. Kamala Das. *My Story* (Delhi : Sterling Publishers, 1976) : 133.
3. Bruce King. *Modern Indian Poetry in English* (Delhi : O.U.P., 1987) : 148.
4. A.N. Dwivedi. *Kamala Das and Her Poetry*. 25.
5. Bruce King. *Modern Indian Poetry in English*. 151.
6. K. Radha. *Kamala Das*, Kerala Writers in English Series : Volume 8 (Madras : Macmillan, 1986) : 6.
7. Kamala Das. *Collected Poems, Vol. 1* (Trivandrum : The Navkerala Printers, 1984). All the references to her collected poems, Vol. 1, abbrevation *CP*, vol. 1.
8. Pritish Nandy. *Indian Poetry in English Today* (New Delhi : Sterling Publishers, 1973) : 121, 122.
9. A.N. Dwivedi. *Kamala Das and Her Poetry*. 5.
10. E.V. Ramakrishnan. 'Death Life's Obscure Parallel' in *Indian Literature Sahitya Academi's Literacy Bi-monthly* (New Delhi : Sahitya Academy Prakashan, No. 115, Sept.-Oct. 1986) : 256-57.
11. Quoted in Raghukul Tilak. *New Indian English Poets and Her Poetry* (Delhi : Rama Brothers Educational Publishers, 1982) : 87.
12. Anisur Rahman. *Expressive Form in the Poetry of Kamala Das* (Delhi : Abhinav Publications, 1981) : 33.
13. Bruce King. *Modern Indian Poetry in English* (Delhi : O.U.P., 1987) : 150.
14. King 149.
15. King 151.
16. Kamala Das. 'Why Not More Than One Husband,' *Eves Weekly*, XXVI 19 (6th May, 1972) : 35.
17. Kamala Das. 'I Have Lived Beautifully,' *Debonair* (15th May, 1975) : 41.
18. Kohli, Devendra. 'Kamala Das' in *Contemporary Indian English Verse — An Evaluation*, ed. Chriantan Kulshreshtha (Delhi : Arnold Heinemann, 1980) : 193.
19. Anisur Rahman. *Expressive Form In the Poetry of Kamala Das*. 23-24.
20. Bruce King. *Modern Indian Poetry in English*. 149.
21. A.N. Dwivedi. *Kamala Das And Her Poetry*. 15.

22. Venugopal, C.V. 'Kamala Das — The Seeker After Truth' in *Living Indian English Poets*, ed. Madhusudan Prasad (Delhi : Sterling Publishers, 1989) : 49.

23. Bruce King. *Modern Indian Poetry in English*. 152-53.

24. King 153.

8

Literary Paradigms of Matriliny : Kamala Das's *My Story*

USHA V.T.*

Most Post-independence Studies on Kerala — in the field of politics, sociology, education or health — have attributed much of Kerala's unique progress to the role of women in both public and private spheres of life. The comparative freedom enjoyed by Kerala women, the social sanctions they were allowed, their educational background and their health and hygiene consciousness were perhaps some of the major reasons for Kerala's dramatic progress. In direct contrast to many of the other States of India, Kerala's birth rate as well as the rate of infant mortality shows marked decline.

What made this tiny State different from the rest of India, was perhaps the unusual importance given to women in its matrilineal societies. In this regard the upper caste Nayars seem to have provided the role model for a vast number of other people to emulate and defend. At a time when the vast majority of Western women suffered oppression in silence and fear, the Kerala women lived in a matrilineal society. Being *matrilocal* (in which the husband lives with the wife's people), their family house granted them security and comfort which their Western counterparts lacked. The women and their children were assured safety and economic well-being even if their male partners defaulted. Divorce was a simple procedure and there was no stigma attached to widowhood or single blessedness. Though the situation was not as ideal as it could

*Department of English, University College, Trivandrum.

have been, the woman's position in society was better than elsewhere in India or abroad. Robin Jeffrey, while trying to expand and illustrate how a combination of politics and women's autonomy has produced the well being associated with Kerala, explains the situation thus :

> Though the system was not matriarchal — women did not govern the household — it accorded them greater freedom, choice and respect than they would have found elsewhere in the world until the twentieth century (35).

Matriliny certainly foregrounded the position of women by tracing descent from a female ancestor or passing on property through the female line. This was in direct opposition to the marginalisation of women in major societies all over the rest of the world.

With the advent of the British and the gradual infiltration of Western patriarchal paradigms, these traditional and indigenous patterns of acceptability came to be viewed as outmoded. The Nayar youths grew ashamed of their time honoured woman-centred society and rushed to pay homage to the patriarchal institutions of their colonial masters. Colonization was largely responsible for depriving Kerala of its matriarchal positions. In the 1810s, the British disarmed the Nayars all over Kerala, and the matrilineal joint-family was forced to cope with peace — an entirely new situation for them. There was a consequent increase in population, and the now jobless young men aspired to be *Karanavans*, creating further confusion. From the 1890s, legislative attempts to reform matriliny began. Kathleen Gough in her exhaustive study, *Matrilineal Kinship*, summarizes the Kerala scene thus :

> Since about 1890, Nayar marriage has become monogamous and men have assumed rights in and obligations to their children. The matrilineage is gradually disintegrating and the elementary family is gradually emerging as the key group in a system of bilateral interpersonal kinship ties (383).

That is to say that the breakdown of matrilineal institutions was an indirect consequence of colonial depredation. One can perceive how it was not merely the economic compulsions, but also the changing social mores that led to the breaking up of matrilineal institutions.

One can consider the autobiography of Kerala's bilingual woman writer Kamala Das as a basic text for study. Kamala Das alias Madhavikutty, who wrote stories in her native Malayalam and poetry in the language of her colonizers, is a member of one of the major matrilineages of Kerala, the Nayar *tharavad*. Her autobiography provides a succinct account of the changing social conditions within the narrow purview of her own *tharavad*, the Nalapat House.

In the process of writing, the self in this work, the poet, herself a victim of colonial depredation, repeatedly resorts to a sort of idealized representation of her *tharavad*. Notwithstanding the fact that there is a certain degree blurring of vision due to the confusion between actual social reality and the poet's idealization of the past, this text provides valuable information about the position of the woman in the Nayar *tharavad*.

The woman in a Nayar *tharavad* is projected as a much respected member of a society that gives her so much economic consideration. She has the freedom to come and go as she pleases or wander around the countryside and even to choose her husband. She explains the circumstances that led to the wedding of her 15-year old ancestress Kunji.

> An aristocrat was to be shown to her at Cochin who was to marry her if she liked his face and if her uncles approved of his deportment (12).

Subsequent circumstances led her elsewhere. But the hypothetical situation where the bride's consent was necessary continued even to the near present. Years later, when the question of Kamala's marriage is raised, she, a mere 15-year old, is the one who makes the choice, allowing herself to be persuaded by the social and financial requirements of her family. There is no coercion involved.

But the woman's voice or choice as the case may be, was definitely secondary to that of her *Karanavan*, her maternal uncle, the patriarch. Kathleen Gough's description of marriage customs among the Nayars explains this situation thus :

> In the 19th century, when monogamy gradually became customary, a *Karanavan* arranged the marriage of his sister's daughter. In earlier period Nayar women seem to have exercised considerable freedom to select or reject their husbands. A woman might not, however, oppose her *Karanavan's* right to dismiss an unwelcome husband.

Kamala Das's description of her granduncle's mother Madhavi Amma illustrates the consequences of this position. Her Valiamma is viewed as an unhappy person with "a great capacity for silence. Kamala reconstructs this person's life story from sketchy details gleaned from the reports of various relatives, quite reluctant to speak of the unfortunate circumstances :

> I learned that Valiamma had been married to a handsome scholar who gave her a son and soon afterwards fell out of favour with her uncle, who threw him out one day asking him never to return.
>
> The Nayars, particularly the males, were coarse when their ire was aroused. The young Brahmin walked away not daring even to glance back once at his wife and scn. The young woman was, within weeks, married off to her father's nephew who was not sensitive or gentle like the one who had gone away. For days she waited at the fence under the lime trees hoping to see her first husband pass that way but he did not (32).

One can see how the pathetic situation described offers a genuine insight into the helplessness of a woman in the matrilineal framework of the Nayar *tharavad*, where the authority of the patriarch or *Karanavan* was final. He was a dictator of sorts, who was expected to look after the basic requirements (like food, shelter, occasional feasts and other forms of entertainment) of his siblings and their offspring. In return, the womenfolk pledged their allegiance to him, accepting his word as final; subverting all contrary pictures of him and idolizing his figure. Kamala Das does the same for her grand uncle Narayana Menon :

> My granduncle Narayana Menon was a famous

> poet-philosopher... he looked every inch a king, although he did not have enough money even to buy the books that he wished to read... At my granduncle's evening durbar there were occasionally brilliant grammarians and writers who came from long distances to stay with him, but they were tongue-tied, and awed by his presence (15).

In this description of her granduncle, Kamala Das is only showing loyalty to her *Karanavan* and taking deep pride in his achievements. This, according to Kathleen Gough, was a common feature of all the Nayars, who "did show great pride in the elders of their *tharavad* as a group, exhibiting their virtues and hiding their weaknesses in the presence of strangers" (349). Though Kamala mentions his weaknesses in her autobiography, it is his strengths that are highlighted.

The presence of unmarried women in the *tharavad* house could be read as an indication of the freedom and sanctions allowed to single women in the Nayar matrilineage. Her aunt Ammini is pictured as an attractive woman with no dearth of proposed suitors, who preferred to adopt Gandhian ways and turn down all marriage proposals. Another example in this category is her portrait of Ammalu, her great grand-mother's younger sister. She remains single though "pretty and eligible" like Ammini, out of her own choice, preferring to deny herself the pleasures of marital bliss, in order to devote her life to poetry and loveliness. The two portraits are ample indication of the lack of stigma attached to spinsterhood in the matrilineal framework of the Nayars, unlike most patriarchal groups.

All these women were educated and could express their thoughts and emotions without restraint if they chose to. By the time the author goes forward in time to her own life, we know that education for women, despite the break-up of matriliny, had come to be accepted as the natural course. As a consequence, they were able to freely express themselves, writing down their emotional inclinations and frustrations. But they rarely went to the extent of publicly declaring their sexual exploits or speaking openly about the shortcomings of life within their *tharavad*. Kamala's forthright confession became an embarrassment to her family and friends in

Kerala as she herself admits in the preface to the autobiography. With the coming in of colonization and the adoption of Western notions of morality, any suggestion of polygamy would be sexual digression and therefore unacceptable. In a society which had now become monogamous accepting patriarchal structures, any effort to return to the subaltern patterns of morality would be an outrage. As she explains,

> My relatives were embarrassed. I had disgraced my well-known family by telling my readers that I had fallen in love with a man other than my lawfully wedded husband.

Divorce, or separation, which was at one time a simple and easy procedure — merely a question to be decided between the individuals concerned and the elders of the family — now became a societal matter. Though the fact that Kamala Das's marriage had "flopped" was obvious, it was not possible for her to initiate measures towards separation for fear of public disapproval. Though divorce and remarriage were not impossible, the whole procedure would not have the social sanction it would have had in earlier times. There was also the question of who would look after the children, for the *tharavad* which had once willingly undertaken to look after the offsprings of its members no longer existed, and the society which was once matrilocal had now become like other patriarchal societies.

> I could not admit to all that my marriage had flopped. I could not return home to the Nalapat House, a divorcee for there had been good-will between our two families for three generations which I did not want to ruin... My parents and other relatives were obsessed with public opinion bothered excessively with our society's reaction to any action of an individual. A broken marriage was as distasteful, as horrifying as an attack of leprosy. If I had at that time listened to the dictates of my conscience and had left my husband, I would have found it impossible to find another who would volunteer to marry me, for I was not conspicuously pretty and besides there was the two-year-old who

> would have been to the new husband an encumbrance (102).

The situation signified the complete breakdown of the structure of the *tharavad* which had once extended security and support to its womenfolk almost unconditionally. All the taboos of the patriarchal institutions had penetrated the sturdy walls of the *tharavad* to bring about its complete destruction; leaving the woman now almost entirely at the mercy of her husband.

The elementary family was torn by two descent groups — that of the husband and that of the wife and children. Yet the prognosis was not as hopeless as the initial implications suggest. Education had given the womenfolk of the matrilineal society a foothold in society that could not be underplayed. This, coupled with the free movement permitted to the womenfolk in the traditionally matrilineal milieu, allowed for gainful employment. As Robin Jeffrey exclaims, "The advantage of Kerala women lay in families' readiness, demonstrated since the 1920s, to send young women into salaried work" (194). Kamala Das herself refers to her writing as a means of income to supplement that of her husband's, for as she indicates in the Preface, she wrote the book during a period of illness when "there were all the hospital bills to be taken care of."

From the above account, it is clear that matriliny provided the basic framework for the uniquely superior position of women in Kerala. Matriliny in Kerala was "humane" (R. Jeffrey), but the woman was not in a position of authority. Yet the structure gave her security and a certain measure or freedom — of choice and action — not available to women in patriarchal societies all over the world. The breakdown of the matrilineal structures in the twentieth century altered this position dramatically, imposing the taboos and restrictions on women in patriarchal societies in these institutions. But the education and social consciousness provided to women by the matrilineal institutions had already provided the foundations which they could individually build upon. Over this basic framework they could act using their personal initiative and vast resources of creative energy to create for themselves a new world of their dreams if they genuinely wished to in a society that was not traditionally averse to their interests or habitually concerned with oppressing them.

9

Split-Self in the Poetry of Kamala Das

SHARADA IYER*

The term Split-Self was first given significance for women's poetry in Flowrence Howe's Introduction to *No More Masks.* It describes an opposition women feel between essential aspects of the self, between what is socially prescribed on the basis of gender and what is defined on the basis of the self, between what a woman feels she should be and what she feels she is. Kamala Das has written a substantial number of poems exploring this duality, the pain and frustrations. She particularly identifies the two selves with the domestic gender role and the artist. The former occupies a safe position accepted and esteemed by society in general and male in particular, while her counterpart haunts the fringes of human intercourse, isolated from men and women alike, and repressed by the women of whose psyche she is a part.

Louis Bernikov notes, "A woman poet constantly pits herself against cultural expectation of 'Womanhood' and 'Woman's Writing.' She gives her imagination and courage to that struggle, pours energy into it in ways that do not exist for men. Womenness is sometimes seen as authenticity, the essence to be distilled in the poems. Sometimes it appears as a blemish the thing to be covered by poems."[1] The result is "women frequently go to self-crippling, self-denying, self-distorting lengths to force themselves into the male sanctioned molds...."[2]

*Head, Department of English, Vasanta College for Women, Rajghat Fort, Varanasi.

Historically women have lacked, been denied opportunities. Connected to the lack of opportunity and training is the fact that women have been denied a judicious critical climate. Speaking of the pervasive presence of male critical and artistic norm that confront the female writer Arienna Rich ironically notes ... the Spectre of ... male judgement along with the active discouragement and thwarting of her need by a culture controlled by male has created problems for the women writers problem of contact with herself, problem of language and style, problem of energy and survival....

Inter-related with the inhibitions and misrepresentation, women have lacked a wealth of subject-matter based on the vitality of their lives. Every woman writer has to deal with the realization that men write out of experience that is 'Universal' but her experience is likely to be regarded as trivial and private. Virginia Woolf also admits the extent of women's censorship of their experience in her delineation of the 'angel in the house' that presiding figure of unimpeachable feminity and propriety who sabotage a women's effort to deal honestly with her feeling. Woolf believed that until a woman writer could 'kill' her 'angel' she would be incomplete in her artistry, hypocritical about her truths. "This compulsiveness, the cause of female socialization, is the perennial enemy of female artists."[3]

This isolation from the subject-matter, from a sense of the importance and legitimacy of their lives is perhaps the most insidious constraint women and women writers face.

"For a woman to attain knowledge and self realization is necessarily to find herself outside a society that ritually and actually enacts loss of self for women. Similarly in modern confessional as an extension of the Adamic tradition the stance of Everyman is readily available to the male poet. It is expected that, personally alienated and desperate as his voice may be, it is still the voice of his time ... yet for the female confessional poet, there is not the same extension. She is not Everyman, and is hardly Everywoman."[4]

Her experience only serves to reinforce her sense of isolation and freakishness. She cannot even believe in a solidarity and community with other women, she would just remain an individual crazy woman.

Women do not look to the golden age in the past, because the past holds no special appeal as a time of harmony and integration for them. Their classic vocation was self-abnegation and their orthodox posture was self-dependency. Women poets acknowledge the human isolation propounded by the existentialists and feel, even within this a further isolation that is unique to the feminine gender. The existentialist feels the gap between the self and other, women feel an additional distance between self and self-expressed most clearly in the sub-genre of split-poems that runs through women's poetry.

The traditional female is associated with the enclosed world of the household. In her guise as a mother, wife and helpmate she exhibits a basic passivity and immobility. The artist however inhabits an unbounded world of independence, movement and vitality. Her freedom and her power can be both stimulating and threatening. Unlike the relatively static domestic self, the artistic choice entails the necessity of confronting unfamiliar experience and environment. Yet the artist appears in clothes and circumstances that stamp her as an indifferent mother, a poor housekeeper, a woman who disregards her social convention keeps her as exotic, eccentric figure. These dichotomies are not unique either in their particular trait or in the split-self strategy, but Kamala Das is worthy of focus for the persistence of the theme in her work, and for the paradigm she presents for examining both the repression and resolution. Her poetry go beyond Stereo-typed longing and complaint. A prominent theme is the need to assert, to conquer, to dominate. Nowhere has the double jeopardy of being a woman and a human being better described than in her poetry.

Anais Nin wrote in her journal what is perhaps one of the most moving statements of the dilemma of conflicting selves in the woman writer, wherein her desire to be loved by man, to be accepted by culture as womanly, rises up to silence the power and voice of the artist.

"I did not want to rival man...I must protect them not outshine them...I did not want to steal man's creation, his thunder. Creation and Feminity seemed in compatible. The aggressive act of creation.

To create seemed such an assertion of the strongest part of me that I would no longer be able to give all these I love the feeling of their being stronger, and they would love me less.

An act of independence would be punished by desertion. I would be abandoned by all those I love....

I have made myself less powerful have concealed my power.

... I have concealed my abilities, like an evil force that would overwhelm, hurt or weaken others.

I have crippled myself.

I have bound myself spiritually.

I have associated creation with ruthlessness, absence of scruples, indifference to consequences.

... The creation guilt in me has to do with feminity, my subjection to men.

Also with my maternal self in conflict with my creative self — Guilt about exposing the father

Secrets
Need of disguises
Fear of Consequences
Great conflict here.[5]

This long, slow cadence of the beginning builds to a litany of confession, a lamentation of loss and mutilation of self in fundamental aspects, maternal and artistic, dutiful and powerful, communal and solitary. These terse almost telegraphic language comes like cries of grief. The grief, the great conflict, of which Nin so eloquently writes flows through the poetry of Kamala Das.

From the beginning Kamala Das demonstrates a continuity of theme and expression concerning central division of the self. Her work is a compelling account of the presence of split. Kamala Das speaks out her heart on her own premises. She redefines herself and liberates herself both as a woman and a poet. She struggles to cope with her problems and dilemmas. She does not attempt to intellectualise, nor does she attempt to spiritualise. She makes a discovery of human existence and narrates her experiences vividly and passionately. She rejects masks and roles and refuses to accept the limitations of her biology.

My grandmother cried
Darling, you must stop this bathing now
you are much too big to play
Naked in the pond.

(*The Descendants*)

The poetry of Kamala Das must be viewed in the light of her feminine consciousness. She acquired this consciousness under hostile circumstances dependent upon the society of her childhood days. Repressive attributes caused fragmentation to her/self. As a poet, she is conscious of her creative faculties and tries to break chains and restraints. She indulges in self-awareness, self-exposure and self-introspection in order to define her self poetically. The aim of the poet is not self-exposure; but self-discovery and self-examination. She structures self-exploration in order to search her lost identity as a woman and as a poet. In a crowded world of men and women she finds herself utterly alone. In poems like *The Freaks, My Grandmother's House, A Hot Noon in Malabar*, *The Sunday Cat, The Invitation* and *The Looking Glass,* she describes an ache growing inside her and disturbing her.

Kamala Das's poetry originates from self which functions like a poetic nucleus. An analysis of her poems reveal that the woman persona of her poems represent her 'own mutilated self' tormented by both past and present and resulting in deep sense of crisis. She feels exploited and cheated by the civilization of which she is a part. Her community, family and civilization expect her to perform the role of a temptress, the goddess, the child and the mother. She has no respect for the culture which has made use of her. She examines her private life because that is the authentic life for her.

The 'Suicide' is a long poem which throws light on the poet's problem of identity. She is disturbed to see the erosion of her personality.

But
I must pose
I must pretend
I must act the role
Of happy woman
Happy wife

I must keep the right distance
Between me and high
I must keep the distance
Between me and the low
O sea, I am fed up
I want to be simple
I want to be loved
And
If love is not be had
I want to be dead....

She finds herself condemned to play the part of the "other." She is not allowed to choose her lot. It is some male who compels her to choose her roles. She is forced to act either as slave or idol. It was never she who chose her lot. She is fed up, grows nostalgic and goes back to the days of her Malabar house.

Kamala Das seems to find no way out of her tormented inner world and knows that there can be no easy solution. Her sense of identity is so fragile that she thinks there are many 'I's' residing within her every thought and impulse claiming its own identity. In "An Introduction" she proclaim

... I am the Sinner
I am a Saint, I am the beloved and the Betrayed,
I have no joys which are not yours, no
Aches which are not yours. I too call myself I.

The painful assertion "I too call myself I" ensues from the typical predicament of being a woman. It is perhaps "the only way to retain her sense of personal worth in the world in categories." It has been rightly pointed out that one poem "Introduction" focuses on "pertinent questions relating to a woman's...identity...."[6]

The portrait of the woman persona that emerges out her poems is a complex one. It is so partly because Kamala Das reveals her feminine sensibility in diverse role such as a wife, beloved, daughter, sister, granddaughter, mother, mistress and even nymphomaniac. "Kamala Das has more to say about the pathos of a woman emerging from a passive role to the point of discovering and asserting her individual freedom and identity...."[7]

"The conflagration" belong to the group of poems that give

voice to the woman's spirit of rebellion against male domination and ego. There is a desire to extricate from this "Soul Killing" subjugation:

"Woman, is this happiness, this lying burried
Beneath a man? It's time again to come alive.
A world extend a Pot beyond his
Six foot frame

The 'Old Play House' also voices her protest against the male domination and the consequent dwarfing of the feminine identity:

Cowering
Beneath your monstrous ego, I
Because a dwarf. I lost my will and reason to all
Questions I mumbled incoherent replies.

Kamala Das caricatures the feminine role to emphasize the plight of being a woman in this world. Her quest for self-knowledge only leads her to the painful realization that is an "Old Playhouse with all its light put out."

The "conflict between passivity and rebellion against the male-oriented universe"[8] is a theme which preoccupies here most. Poems such as "The Proud One," "Captive," "Substitute," "The Conflagration" enable us to witness the transition from passivity to rebellion. In her poems she examines "the psychic disintegration which results, when self rejects established norms." The psychological trauma, frustrations and the resultant quest for identity and wholeness is a result of the revolt against male dominated world and society. Kamala Das's poetry underline the predicament of contemporary woman beset by the crisis of divided selves. Her aims as a poet is to bring about harmony out of her existence. Though such a harmonious state is never found, the attempt goes on. The poems are remarkable because they reveal here feeling of anxiety, alienation, meaninglessness, futility, acute sense of isolation, fragmented self and loss of identity.

There is a dualism in her writing. The dualism results from the fall from childhood innocence into the adult world of sexuality, marriage and life among strangers, especially an uncaring husband. "The interest of Das's poetry is not the story of sex outside of marriage but the instabilitv of her feelings, the way they rapidly shift and assume new postures, new attitude of defence, attack, explanation or celebration. Her poems are situated neither in the act of sex nor in the feeling of love, they are instead involved with the self and its varied, often conflicting emotions, ranging from the desire for security and intimacy to the assertion of the ego, self-dramatization and feeling of shame and depression."[9]

Confessional poets court death and disintegration as well as psychic wholeness and insights. This tension between two opposites is reflected in the constantly shifting moods of confessional poetry. "Composition" embraces such diverse moods as passionate attachment, agonizing guilt, nauseating disgust and inhuman bitterness. Images of deep involvement in the physical act of love are followed by those of physical rotting, disgust and sickness in poems like "The Old Playhouse," "In Love," "Gino." An extreme point is reached when she distrusts the very medium of poetry and laments its artificiality:

> I have stretched my two dimensional
> Nudity on Sheets of weeklies, monthlies
> Quarterlies, a sad sacrifice, I have
> Put my private voice away, adopted the
> Typewriter's click as my only speech.

Kamala Das is essentially a poet of the modern Indian women's ambivalence. She seems to have a good deal of the conventional woman in her make up, so that not only can she speak of the common woman and her basic need for love and security with inside knowledge, but cannot help, in addition expressing an ambivalence proceeding from her own duality the combination in herself of a need for domestic security and the desire for independence, an independence not consistent with a domestic mode of living.

The *Split-self* poem deals primarily with a sense of isolation a poet feels between her social female self and the inner artistic self. The poet in these poems may have more sense of functioning positively in the world, yet they do so with an awareness of duality. The external socially acceptable integrated feminine woman co-exists with the internal or rebellious, unfeminine isolated artist, who is not acceptable, acting and opposing in ways defiant of social approval. Poets like Kamala Das who is capable of being a positive even celebratory of human relationship, has woven throughout her work a series of poems describing herself as two co-existent women — who are in varying degree of tension with each other. The artist and the women seem necessarily estranged.

REFERENCES

1. Louis Bernikov. Introduction in Berkinow *The World Splits Open : Four Centuries of Women Poets in England and America 1551-1950* (N.Y. 1974) : 8.
2. Susan Koppelman Cornillon. *The Fiction of Fiction* in Cornillon (ed.). *Images of Women in Fiction* (Bowling Green, Ohio, 1973) : 114.
3. Erica Jung. 'Writing As a Woman,' *Book View* (April 1978) : 21.
4. Sandra Gilbert. "My Name is Darkness, The Poetry of Self Definition," *Contemp. Lit.* XIX, 1978 : 443-57.
5. Entry for Jan. 1943, The Diaries of Anais Nin, Vol. III, cited in Jeanette Webber and Joan Grumman (ed.). *Woman as Writer,* (Boston, 1978) : 36-37.
6. Kohli, Devendra. *Kamala Das* (New Delhi : Arnold-Heinemann, 1975) : 188.
7. Devendra 29.
8. Barbara Segnity and Carol Rainey. *Introduction to Psyche, The Feminine Poetic Consciousness,* N.Y., 1973, quoted by Devendra Kohli in Kulshreshtha (ed.). *Contemporary Indian English Verse.* 190.
9. Bruce King. *Modern Indian Poetry in English* (OUP, 1987) : 149-51.

10

Between the Fire and the Hungry Earth : A Note on Kamala Das

K. INDRA SENA REDDY*

Of all the Indian-English women poets, Kamala Das has received maximum critical attention. More often than not, she has been acknowledged and acclaimed as an outstanding love-poet. Her poetry, in the main, deals with the various facets of love-experience. It is interesting to note that Kamala Das's love obsession has an undercurrent of melancholy feeling for death. This aspect of her poetry dealing with the theme of death merits critical examination. An attempt is made in this paper to analyse how death theme manifests itself in varied forms and how it operates at different levels.

The poet's frequent illness and confinement to hospital for long spells set in a sort of realization as to the inevitability and universality of death. She observes : "Often I heard from different parts of the hospital women moaning, grieving over the death of some relative."[1] She has said in "Gino" :

> ...I dream of obscene hands
> Striding up my limbs and of morgues where
> the night-lights
> Glow on faces shuttered by the soul's exit. And
> long corridors

*Professor of English, University of Asmara, Asmara, Eritrea.

To the X-ray room's dark interior.
(O, the clatter of the trolleys, with the
dead on them,
As loud as untimely laughter)...........

The interplay of light and darkness reinforces the sense of death. The "Night-lights" in the "morgues" glowing on faces "shuttered by the soul's exit" are expressive of the eerie halo surrounding a dead body. The white-robed ward-boys are "sepulchral" death messengers. "The dark interior" of the "X-ray rooms" has the overtones of the possible mysterious revelations of death and "the clatter of trolleys" with dead bodies produces weird sound effects. This unnatural noise of death like untimely laughter emanates from darkness itself.

It is not the hospital atmosphere alone that provides her moments to contemplate death. Quite a few ordinary facts of experience set her thinking with metaphysical vividness. She muses "the boundaries of/Paradise had shrunk to a mere/Six by two" (The Invitation). Whatever be the metaphysical dimensions of a paradise, the bare truth of its physical measure is just 'six' by 'two.' That is what a sinner or saint requires or gets at the end.

The sights at the seashore and the tombs at the cemeteries make her feel the pervasive death in every town and in every house. "Blood" conveys poignantly her obsession with death theme.

From every town I live in
I hear the rattle of its death
the noise of rafters creaking
and the windows' whine

It is characteristic of Kamala Das that she churns deathly feeling out of an ordinary event like the "whining" of "windows" and the "creaking" of "rafters." The awareness of death leads her to its acceptance and she prepares herself to face it squarely. She gradually sheds the fear-psychosis usually associated with death and musters "enough courage to die" (The Suicide). Further, she presents the view that Death makes itself felt in the descent of darkness each night :

Each night when darkness turns
Me blind, I think of death,

Understanding it to
Be like night-fall, Just a
Temporary phase, which
Brings no loss... (Death Brings No Loss).

Death is like a night-fall while the darkness causes only a temporary lapse of vision but no real deprivation.

Emily Dickinson's poem "Because I could not Stop for Death" may be contrasted with this poem on the problem of death. The poet visualises a jolly ride in the company of Death to the graveyard. She believes that she is all set and well prepared to walk into the waiting hands of Death :

We slowly drove, he knew no haste,
And I had put away
My labour, and my leisure too,
For his civility :

In contrast to this casual response to the call of death, Emily Dickinson realizes to her dismay that she is overwhelmed with a sense of shock at the striking power of death as the poem progresses. She becomes aware that all her preparations to embrace death have been too inadequate. It is, perhaps, not without some significance, that she also ensures the company of Immortality as a fellow-traveller in order to take the sting out of Death :

The carriage held just ourselves
And Immortality.

Notwithstanding a facade of fearlessness intended to be displayed by the poet, the concluding lines of the poem are marked by an abrupt shift both in terms of meaning and the course of the journey :

I first surmised the horses' heads were towards eternity.

The poet, tries to persuade herself that the journey will progress beyond the frontiers of death so as to cruise her to the secure territory of eternity.

The contrast between the two poems is that while Emily Dickinson opts for death but at the same time looks for an escape, Kamala Das transcends the fear of death and looks at it as a casual and routine affair and as a matter of little significance and "no loss."

Kamala Das views death with a sense of detachment, and considers life "as a slow yielding to the 'cold loveliness' of death."[2] She concedes that the assaults of time, like the gradual assaults of love, yield to the slow dissolution of death. She is able to take to death like a maiden who surrenders to her lover, or like a child who gives himself to the mother's arms :

...We were the yielders,
Yielding ourselves to everything. It is
....
...not for us even to
Question death, but as child to mother's arms
We shall give ourselves to the fire or to
The hungry earth to be slowly eaten,
Devoured... (The Descendants).

The poet seems to be of the view that challenging the power and inevitability of death is an exercise in futility. Death is mysterious. It chooses its own time to strike and manifests itself on its own terms. The ultimate reality is that every human body will either be consumed by the flames or devoured by the hungry earth.

It is characteristic of the poet that she often juxtaposes death with the ordinary incidents of living. In "My Son's Teacher," she weaves into the texture of the poem the fact of the death of the teacher, the noise, revelry and jubilation of those partaking in a procession and the blissful innocence of the child who neither understands nor feels the significance of the event :

My son is four. His teacher swooned on a
grey pavement
Five miles from here and died. From where
she lay, her new skirt
Flapped and fluttered, a green flag,
half-mast, to proclaim death's
Minor triumphs...
....
Long gaudy processions, they clapped
cymbals, they beat drums

and They sang aloud, she who lay in a faint
was drowned
In their song....

The poor teacher faints and breathes her last on a public pavement. While "Death" proclaims with pride her "minor triumphs," the dead lay on the pavement unwept and unlamented. Against this background of death, the celebrations of the 'Vinayak Chathurthi' are carried on with pomp and show. The poet's son who is four years of age, "Bathed, drank milk. Wrote two crooked lines of/ Ds and waited." The child in his innocence does not know the reasons for the absence of his teacher.

Kamala Das's obsession with death keeps haunting her even while she serves wine :

...I shall serve wine
In glasses cold like a dead man's palm
I shall serve a blood-red cherry wine
(The White Flowers)

She is haunted by the loneliness of death even in the midst of a mundane experience — whether the occasion is a cock-tail party or an equally insignificant event. "In Love" and "The Wild Bougainvillea" also deal with the same theme. While "In Love" points out the inadequacy of sex-experience to the extent of forcing her to join the mourners at

Night, from behind the Burdwan
Road, the corpse-bearers cry 'Bol
Hari Bol....'

"The Wild Bougainvillea" presents the sight of the dead whose tombstones have been changed beyond recognition with the names of the dead erased by the rains and the assaults of time.

The poet elaborates in "Nani" how the dead are sought to be put out of our minds :

...Each truth
Ends thus with a query. It is this designed
Deafness that turns Mortality into
Immortality, the definite
Into the soft indefinite.....

Nani, the maid servant, commits suicide by hanging. The poet who was only a child at that time imagines as the dead body turns round on the rope that she (The maid servant) "Was doing, to delight us, a comic/Dance...." In course of time, the poet's grandmother forgets all about Nani, but Kamala Das does not. Perhaps, the old woman does not want the child's mind to be haunted by the thoughts about the dead. The "deafness" on the part of the grandmother is "designed" and it is also a conscious attempt to forget the dead. Paradoxically, the deliberate attempt to forget all that is unpleasant in life makes us all the more conscious of it. The very act of forgetting leads us to the reality of remembrance which cannot be easily put out of our minds. She emphasises that "a truth forgotten, a fact overlooked is what makes the truth doubly memorable."[3] It is this "designed deafness" the turns "mortality into immortality," the "definite" into the "soft indefinite."

A few poems in *The Old-Play House and Other Poems*, and many more included in *The Descendants* as well as those in *The Summer In Calcutta* are heavily stuffed with the vocabulary of "dying," "funeral-pyre," "half-burnt logs," "dead," "tomb," "crucifixion," "corpses," "buried" and the list can be stretched to any length. At times, one is struck with the feeling that there is so much of fever, sickness, rotting and death in the poetry of Kamala Das, that one is provoked to assail her for the conspicuous absence of compassion which is "an indispensable quality of a genuinely important poet."[4]

The frequency with which she uses the 'sea' image in the poems of *The Descendants* testifies to her persistent penchant for death :

> The Sea is garrulous today. Came in,
> Come in. What do you lose by dying, ...
> (The Invitation)

Not only does the sea invite her repeatedly to join her but it also seeks to convince her that she loses nothing by dying. She realises how futile it would be to reject the friendly offer of the sea. She makes up her mind despite initial hesitation to accept the invitation as it is too tempting to resist. She asks herself, "How long can one resist?"

In "Substitute," the poet turns to 'night' and begs of it to restore peace to her so as to enable her to lie quietly :

> Let me lie still
> Without thought or will,
> For a benign hour or two,
> Dear night, be my tomb.

The poet craves for the silence, peace and tranquillity of the quiet night in order to ensure for herself a lasting sense of relief from the burdensome life. The poetry of Kamala Das, particularly, the poems included in *Summer In Calcutta* explore, in the words of Srinivasa Iyengar, "this theatre of enervation, this vestibule of unresolved tension,"[5] and the death itself through the images of the sea, the decaying body, rotting garbage and the dead fish so intensely that her poetry, at times, reads like the fever-chart of a hopeless case. However, the fever-chart of Kamala Das's poetry is not without its silver lining as the following lines illustrate :

> Morning tree, on your brown bony branch, one day,
> I shall see a sudden flower, and know at once
> That my death is just a flower....
>
> (My Morning Tree)

Kamala Das, despite her patent obsession with death, is not negative in her attitude to it. She is, in fact, able to visualise in death the tremendous potentialities of a creative force. She not only envisions her death as a 'flower,' emphasising her acceptance of it, but reveals her ability to glorify death as a rich experience.

REFERENCES

1. Kamala Das. *My Story* (New Delhi : Sterling Publishers, 1976) : 151.
2. Kohli, Devendra. *Kamala Das* (New Delhi : Arnold-Heinemann Publishers, 1975) : 100.
3. Devendra 107.
4. Monika Verma. *Facing Four* (Calcutta : Writers Workshop, 1973) : 33.
5. Iyengar, K.R. Srinivasa. *Indian Writing in English* (Bombay : Asia Publishing House, 1973) : 677.

11

Suffering and Humiliation in Kamala Das's Poetry

K.V. SURENDRAN*

In her autobiography *My Story*, Kamala Das has maintained that poets "cannot close their shops like shopmen and return home. Their shop is their mind and as long as they carry it with them they feel the pressures and the torments. A poet's raw material is not stone or clay, it is her personality" (1977 : 165). One can easily see that though Kamala Das is speaking about poets in general whatever she says is equally applicable to her also. She is one of the most aggressively individualistic of the poets writing in India. She has poetry in her blood; both her mother and grandfather being established poets in Malayalam.

The world of her poems is thoroughly Indian or a world that she has made her own. But more than the Indianness what strikes one most in her poems is the feminine sensibility. "Kamala Das did display tremendous courage in revolting against the sexual colonialism and providing hope and confidence to young women that they can refuse and reject the victim positions, that they can frustrate the sexist culture's effort to exploit, passivise and marginalise women" (Kaur : 1996 : 232). Her main concern happens to be suffering and humiliation meted out to women. This paper is an attempt to have a close look at some of her poems where she successfully deals with this theme.

One of the important poems where Kamala Das draws our

***Institute of English and Foreign Languages, Kannur University, Thalassery Campus, Palayad, Thalassery, Kannur, Kerala.**

attention to the sufferings and humiliation which women are made to experience is "Nani." The focus of the poem is a pregnant housemaid hanging herself, an act to which she was driven by shame and moral austerity of the society in which she lived. The spectacle of Nani hanging from a rope is heart-rending which raises unanswerable questions :

> Nani, the pregnant maid, hanged herself
> In the privy one day. For three long hours
> Until the police came, she was hanging there
> A clumsy puppet, and when the wind blew
> Turning her gently on the rope;
>
> (*The Best of Kamala Das* : 19)

The image of the clumsy puppet performing a comic dance is noted for its vividness and also for its suggestiveness. Nani, as is made evident by the poet, has been a puppet in the hands of fate and the real culprit who has subjected her to such humiliation is of course the society and also its moral codes. She hangs from a rope as a helpless victim to the designs of an "unknown citizen" and the effect produced to the eyes of children is comic!

> ....it seemed
> To us who were children then, that Nani
> was doing, to delight us, a comic Dance.
>
> (*BK* : 19)

The grandmother in the poem, after a year or two parries the unpleasant question when the speaker asks her whether she remembers Nani. She also can only be part of a society which has its own ways and it is not an unexpected response that the speaker receives from her. That is why the speaker has a readymade answer to why she reacts in that way.

> Each truth
> Ends thus with a query. It is designed
> Deafness that turns mortality into
> Immortality, the definite into
> The soft indefinite.
>
> (*BK* : 19)

As far as the speaker is concerned, the experience appears to have been one of initiation. She moves from a world of innocence to a narrow, conservative way of life which prefers to suppress what is unpleasant and "unexposable."

In her poem "Advice to Fellow-Swimmers" Kamala Das advises her fellow men to learn how to swim. The poem is a powerful lyric with a strong philosophical undercurrent. She considers life as an everflowing stream which ends up the ocean, that is, the infinite.

> When you learn to swim
> do not enter a river that has no ocean
> to flow into one ignorant of destinations
> and knowing only the flowing as its destiny.
>
> (*Collected Poems* : Volume 1 : 100)

The obvious message is that one should have a goal ahead and that one should not be tied down by the means. She also wants to underscore the point that purposeless swimming leads to suffering and agitation. Perhaps she has in her mind the toiling masses around her who lead a meaningless life full of suffering. She wants to emphasize the fact that one's ultimate aim should be to overcome one's own self so that ultimately it will be an escape from suffering. It is liberation from the self that brings joy and peace :

> go swim in the great blue sea
> where the first tide you meet is your body,
> that familiar pest;
> but if you learn to cross it
> you are safe, yes, beyond it you are safe,
> for, even sinking would make no difference then....
>
> (*Collected Poems* : Volume 1 : 100)

Kamala Das compares the body to a familiar pest, that is, a troublesome or destructive thing. The body is troublesome in so far as it is matterbound and hence subject to many limitations. If the temptations of the body are overcome, the soul will attain freedom, she thinks. At another level, the poem is an appeal to her fellow women to break the shell in which they are, no more to be passive and discover and assert their individual freedom and identity putting an end to constant suffering and humiliations in a society known for its patriarchal designs.

The poem "My Son's Teacher" also is noted for suffering

though at a different level. It deals with the death of a teacher, a minor tragedy enacted on the crowded pavement of the city.

His teacher swooned
On a grey pavement
Five miles from here and died.

(*Indian Poetry in English Today* : 89)

The mother keeps the tragedy from her son and he goes on waiting for the usual door bell. In fact it will be in great mental agony that the child will be engaged in the long wait which is never going to fructify.

...th
Bathed, drank milk, wrote two lines of 'D's
and waited.
But the dead rang no door bell.

(*Indian Poetry in English Today* : 89-90)

In fact the child is too young to know the full significance of the tragedy. But the fact remains that suffering has been inflicted on the young mind by its own mother by not revealing to him the exact state of affairs :

He is only four.
For many years he will not be told that tragedy.

(*Indian Poetry in English Today* : 90)

The boy is unaware of the intrusion of death into his life and the poem ends with a moving image of tragedy where an old sad bird gently touches his shoulder with its wing. Perhaps after years he would know that the bird of death had flown over him that afternoon, tenderly touching him with its wing-tip.

"Middle Age" is a poem which surveys the little, unnoticed pangs of mothers who are already on the "wrong side of the forties." She begins the poem telling us when a person can be called middle aged.

Middle age is when your children are no longer
Friends but critics, stern of face and severe with
their tongue

(*Symphony* : 26)

The situation she describes here is one that is common place and found in every other household. When children grow up estrangement develops and the views of the old generation becomes totally unacceptable to the growing generation. The ultimate result is that the elderly people are made to suffer for no fault of theirs. The modern solution to this problem is nuclear families where the grey haired are mercilessly banished. Even when they get an entry to the households their role is limited to providing amenities to the other inmates of the house, that is, the role of a servant.

....they no longer
Need you except for serving tea and for
pressing
clothcs

(*Symphony* : 26)

Certainly it is a life of humiliation and suffering that the middle aged are made to experience. Like a pupa becoming a cocoon and then butterfly, the silent obedient child has all on a sudden become an independent self-asserting personality and the casualty is his own mother. The poet's attempt in this poem is to wake up the dreamy middle aged mothers and to prepare them face the ultimate reality shedding the mental torture that has been in store for them :

You have lived
In a dream world all your life, it's time to
Wake up, Mother,
You are no longer so young you know

(*Symphony* : 26)

"My Grandmother's House" reveals Kamala Das's nostalgic yearning for her family home, Nalappat House, in Malabar, Kerala. She remembers the house where she received love and affection from her grandmother. But one will not miss the dominant tone of despair and suffering in this poem also :

How often I think of going
There, to peer through the blind eyes of
windows or
Just listen to the frozen air,
Or in wild despair, pick an armful of
Darkness to bring it here to lie

Behind my bedroom door like a brooding
Dog.

(*BK* : 21)

The poet takes note of the change that has come over in the house after her grandmother's death. She realizes that the house has withdrawn to silence which should make her also suffer in silence. The house has boasted of a great personal library and her incapacity to read the books as a child brings only regrets to her mind. This is certainly an agonising thought as far as the poet is concerned. Out of sheer despair, she wishes to pick an armful of darkness from there to her present place of abode. She is unable to proceed with her thoughts for sometime all because of the mental torture. She finds herself reduced to the status of a beggar with the only difference that she stretches her arms for love. She feels insecure because of the mental suffering and is made to move to desolation and frigidity.

I who have lost
My way and beg now at stranger's doors to
Receive love, at least in small change?

(*BK* : 21)

We find that in this poem Kamala Das is concerned with herself as a victim. In a sense she is able to transform her intense personal experience into a general truth. That is because, whatever she tries to communicate here has a universal appeal and the readers never fail to 'feel' her mental suffering when they go through the poem.

Kamala Das's "A Hot Noon in Malabar" is also known for an atmosphere that is hostile and unpleasant. When others are annoyed by the heat, dust and noise, the poet longs for the hot noon in Malabar because it is associated with "wild men, wild thoughts, wild love."

Yes, this is
A noon for wild men, wild thoughts, wild love To
Be here, far away, is torture. Wild feet
Stirring up the dust, the hot noon, at my
Home in Malabar, and I so far away....

(*BK* : 18)

A hot noon in Malabar is a time when strangers are welcome. They come from the sun to peer into the rooms, but the brightness of the sun temporarily dims their eyesight. The environment is hostile and the strangers look around with mistrust in their eyes :

.... This
Is a noon for strangers with mistrust in
Their eyes, dark, silent ones who rarely speak
At all....

(*BK* : 18)

The poet in such an atmosphere yearns for the spontaneity which was present in that early life as a child in Malabar. She is sick of the routine when everything is mechanical. She believes that the only way out of the suffering is to travel down memory lane, that is to her life as a child in Malabar.

In "The Sunshine Cat" Kamala Das speaks of the injustice meted out to women where again the dominant motif is suffering. She believes that the society is hostile to women and that they are humiliated in all possible ways. A man is free to go in search of love and her own husband whom she loved, did not love in return :

They did this to her, the men who knew her, the man
She loved, who loved her not enough, being selfish
And a coward, the husband who neither loved nor
Used her, but was a ruthless watcher, and the band
Of cynics she turned to, clinging to their chests where
New hair sprouted like great-winged moths,
borrowing her
Face into their smells and their young lusts to forget,
To forget oh, to forget....

(*Ten Twentieth Century Indian Poets* : 25)

She seems to lose her sanity when she is forced on to the bed against her desire as bed is no more a place that can offer her comfortable sleep :

They let her slide from pegs of sanity into
A bed made soft with tears and she lay there weeping,
For sleep had lost its use....

(*Ten Twentieth Century Indian Poets* : 25)

To escape from the suffering and humiliation all she can do is to build a wall :

.... I shall build walls with tears
She said, walls to shut me in....

(*Ten Twentieth Century Indian Poets* : 25)

But after her middle ages he realizes that she has lost all her vitality. The poem is a strong representation of the feelings of Indian women who are very often mere puppets in the hands of the ever dominating men. They are like "flies to wanton boys" to be thrown away after the "operation." They continue to be illtreated and humiliated by men till they are sure that they are no more of use to them and are mere "half-dead" creatures.

The eunuchs are destined to lead a life of endless suffering and the poem "The Dance of the Eunuchs" is about the desperate eunuchs who have nothing to look forward to. It is a meaningless dance that they are engaged in even when they lead a barren life :

... Beneath the fiery gulmohur, with
Long braids flying, dark eyes flashing,
they danced, and
They danced, oh, they danced till they bled
... There were green
Tattoos on their cheeks, jasmines in their,
hair, some
Were dark and some where almost fair.

(*BK* : 60)

Though they sing melancholic of dying lovers and unborn children, they fail to produce any sympathy as their voices are harsh and also because they indulge in their dance only with vacant ecstasy. The eunuchs are as good as half-burnt logs of woods taken from funeral pyres, according to the poet :

.... They
Were thin in limbs and dry; like half-burnt
legs from
Funeral pyres, a drought and a rottenness
Were in each of them.

(*BK* : 60)

Again the focus is on sterility of their body and they survive only to suffer, humiliated and ridiculed by a hostile world. They are sheer misfits in such a world and the poet successfully draws the attention of the society to their pathetic life.

"An Introduction" is a poem where Kamala Das tells us why she prefers to write in English.

I am Indian, very brown, born in
Malabar, I speak three languages, write in
Two, dream in one. Don't write in English,
they said,
English is not your mother-tongue. Why not leave
Me alone, critics, friends, visiting cousins,
Everyone of you? Why not let me speak in
Any language I like? The language I speak
Becomes mine, its distortions, its queernesses
All mine, mine alone....

(*BK* : 12)

Language is a sensitive issue and in this poem the language becomes the bone of contention. Obviously, there is some resistance from certain quarters about her writing in a language of her choice. For her it is more than a mental torture to listen to instructions from others as to which language she should write in and also speak. As Iyengar remarks "the endless reiteration of such hurt, such disillusion, such cynicism, must sooner or later degenerate into a mannerism." (1985 : 680)

To put it briefly, suffering and humiliation are undoubtedly the dominating themes in Kamala Das's poetry in the poems taken up for discussion. She airs her views with a boldness unparalleled and she hopes that the society might change their attitude to those who suffer and are humiliated. She is essentially a poet of the modern Indian woman's ambivalence, giving expression to it more openly than any other Indian Woman poet. "Kamala Das's poetry has her autobiography written into it. She is not any woman or the incarnation of "Essential Womanhard" if at all there is one : She is an Indian poet, writing in English when Indian poetry in English is breaking free from the rhetorical and romantic traditions when her male counterparts like Nissim Ezekiel and A.K. Ramanujan are struggling hard to form a dense, pitty and ironic idiom in their poems and Jayanta Mahapatra is trying to relate his poetry to his immediate environment with pain and anger" (Satchidanandan : 1996 : 9).

REFERENCES

Das, Kamala. *My Story*. New Delhi : Sterling Publishers Pvt. Ltd., 1977.

——. *Collected Poems*. Volume I, Trivandrum, 1984.

——. *The Best of Kamala Das*. Kozhikode : Bodhi Publishing House, 1991.

——. "Middle Age," *Symphony*. Calicut : University of Calicut, 1995.

Iyengar, K.R. Srinivasa. *Indian Writing in English*. New Delhi : Sterling Publishers Pvt. Ltd., 1985.

Kaur, Iqbal. "Protest Against Sexual Colonialism : Kamala Das's *My Story,*" *Women's Writing : Text and Context*, ed. Jasbir Jain. New Delhi : Rawat Publications, 1996.

Nandy, Pritish. *Indian Poetry in English Today*. New Delhi : Sterling Publishers Pvt. Ltd., 1981.

Parthasarathy, R. (ed.). *Ten Twentieth Century Indian Poets*. Delhi : OUP, 1984.

Satchidanandan, K. "Transcending the Body," *Only the Soul Knows How to Sing*, Kottayam : D.C. Books, 1996.

12

Kamala Das and the Confessional Mode

N. RAMADEVI*

Kamala Das writes with a frankness and openness unusual in the Indian context. Most Indian poets in English do not have the candour of Kamala Das in creatively analysing and evaluating their experience. Just as the American confessional poets such as Sylvia Plath and Anne Sexton she exploits the confessional mode in order to discover the images that evoke the joy and frustration of achieved womanhood.

Confessional mode of writing has its virtual origin in the mid 50s in America, John Berryman, Robert Lowell, Anne Sexton, Sylvia Plath being its chief exponents. Confessional poetry is a hybrid mode of poetry that came into existence as a consequence of the popularization of the psychological studies, the spread of the Freudian and Jungian theories, and the emergence of the feminist movement. Confessional poetry means objective, analytical or even clinical observation of incidents from one's own life whether tinged with comedy or irony, self loathing or compassion. One thing that these writers have in common is the conception of the self as passive : the confessional poets alternately flagellate and flaunt, punish and cosset themselves. They see themselves as victims and heroes — sufferers through their sensitivity, heroic in their suffering which renders a peculiar tone — or rather range of tones — nervous and hardboiled, sullen and self-pitying, the nervous breakdown often ending up in suicide. Suicide as the guarantor of integrity and the procurer of authenticity is the true

*Lecturer in English, S.K. University, Anantapur, Andhra Pradesh.

identifying preoccupation of the school. The chaos of the psychic situation becomes the ground of a reoriented art in which the beset self is the testing ground and the embodiments of all human possibilities — the terrors, pains, early miseries, regrets, vexations, (and lassitudes) remain as the proofs of one's existence, the degree of the intensity confirming one's reality. "The artistic problem is to make a genuine poetry out of the language of untrammeled self-awareness."[1]

Kamala Das, who writes in the tradition of confessional writers indulges in a great deal of heartbaring. "The poetry never reaches a stage of sickness and breakdown but in her morbid moods Kamala Das comes close to the more pathological states of confessional poetry when she steers clear of self-pity on the one hand, and the exhibitionism on the other, she is profoundly moving, and the loneliness and despair come through."[2] Self-pity and exhibitionism are somewhat unpoetic; but loneliness and despair are poetic. Kamala Das seems to be profound when she makes loneliness and despair come through.

Most of the poems by Kamala Das are explorations of the gender roles an Indian woman plays — the embarrassment they involve, the resistance they provoke, and the pain they cause. The confessional mode in Kamala Das is a dramatisation of the self, to place itself in focus with itself. The confessional mode becomes a device to formalize the process of analysis and adjustment of the problems that crop up from arranged marriage at an early age. She confesses in her autobiography, *My Story*[3] all her frustrations, doubts, and anxieties stem from her early marriage.

A desperate obsession with love is one of the prominent features of Kamala Das's poetry. The failure to arrive at it leaves her in the claustrophobic world of the self, the wounded self. "The Freaks," "The Old Playhouse," "An Introduction," "The Looking Glass," are some poems in which the wounded self, which has to struggle hard to achieve its own identity, is not only the central theme but the principle of organisation as such. Erotic indulgence keeps the self within the orbit of a relationship without making it lament over its wounds. Isolation leads to despair through fear. In "The Freaks," the speaker says : "who can help us who have lived so long and have failed in love." The speaker says that she is a freak and the freakishness is an internalization of the speaker's urgently felt need to save her face.

"The Old Playhouse" seems to provide the key to her dialectical attitude to the male-oriented discourse, and helps the reader familiarize himself / herself with the poet's complex calculus associated with love and lust. The title of the poem constitutes its central image, and the speaker feels that love-making has made her mind an "Old Playhouse with all its lights put out." The self is blocked and choked, and it finds itself in a state of emotional darkness. The man is presented as a deliberate tactician in taming a free bird, his plans succeed in making the bird forget her nature, *i.e.* the urge to fly. The male ego reduces her to the level of a dwarf. Her contact with him makes her aware of her body, which is not an asset to her but a liability.

"Of Calcutta" is a poem which, besides making a general reference to the gender roles, specifies the essence of a wounded self in an angry mood wherein she refers to her residence as "my husband's home." The image of a "trained circus dog" makes obvious the sort of home in which she stays. But she does not forget to ask, "Where is my soul, my spirit, where the muted tongues of my desire?" Her creative concern seems to find her soul, her spirit, to articulate her muted desire and thus to make herself in the process of which she learns the poetics of confessional mode.

Although Kamala Das seems to be intensely aware of the self, the critical consideration is whether she has succeeded in discerning appropriate language and structure to communicate it.

"An Introduction" is one poem the analysis of which seems to clarify doubts as to the poet's capacity to discover an adequate linguistic medium.

The poem has a double theme; it deals with the language of identity and the identity of a woman as a woman. Like most poems of Kamala Das, "An Introduction" begins with a statement :

> I don't know politics but I know the names
> Of those in power, and can repeat them like
> Days of week, or names of months, beginning with
> Nehru. I am Indian, very brown, born in

Malabar, I speak three languages, write in
Two, dream in one. Don't write in English, they said,
English is not your mother-tongue. Why not leave
Me alone, critics, friends, visiting cousins,
Every one of you? Why not let me speak in
Any language I like? The language I speak
Becomes mine, its distortions, its queernesses
All mine, mine alone. It is half English, half
Indian, funny perhaps, but it is honest,
It is as human as I am human, don't
You see?

("An Introduction," 1-15)

A mild sort of irritation and an anxiety to assert one's hold over the medium of articulation are combined to create a strongly felt need to confess and to communicate. The success of the confessional poems seems to depend on the honesty of the self and the inquiring mind's integrity in thought, feeling, and creation and Kamala Das impresses by being very much herself in her poems. English Language, as the speaker of the poem unemphatically and without any sort of irony, says,

Is human speech, the speech of the mind that is
Here and not there, a mind that sees and hears and
Is aware.

("An Introduction," 18-20)

What the speaker tells us is that she has a mind that sees, hears, and is aware. The task of a poet is to find a linguistic structure and a frame of reference to communicate what he or she sees, hears, and is aware of. This creative urge leads to a confession of the speaker's experience as a married woman, not exactly knowing what marriage is, and what it demands of her as a woman :

I was child, and later they
Told me I grew, for I became tall, my limbs
Swelled and one or two places sprouted hair. When
I asked for love, not knowing what else to ask
For, he drew a youth of sixteen into the
Bedroom and closed the door. He did not beat me
But my sad woman-body felt so beaten.

("An Introduction," 23-29)

The lines reveal the fact that the poet's early marriage seems to have given a rude jolt to her sensibility as a woman. The "he" of the poem did not beat her, but her "sad woman-body felt so beaten." The speaker seems to consider her "sad woman-body" as the source of trouble. It appears to be a very humiliating experience. For a woman, her body seems to stand in the way of establishing her identity. To revive the self from the humiliating experience, the speaker changes her dress, wears a shirt and trousers, cuts her hair short, ignores her womanliness. The categorizers think that her behaviour smacks of a rebellion against male authority. They advise her, "Dress in Sarees, be girl / Be wife, they said. Be embroiderer, be cook, / Be a quarreller with servants. Fit in, oh, / Belong ("An Introduction," 33-36).

In most Indian homes a young house-wife is expected to be an embroiderer, a cook, and a manager of the domestic establishment. She is not expected to "sit on walls or peep through lace draped windows." She has to be identified with a name. "Be Amy or be Kamala or, better / still, be Madhavikutty" ("An Introduction," 38-39).

Suppose a house-wife is not at peace with herself or with her husband society would tell her to play ''pretending games" like, a schizo or a nympho. Till this point, the poem is a mild satire on the male attitudes and the conventional gender role assigned to a wife in terms of the dos and don'ts. From this the rest of the poem follows as the mild protest of a woman who very much wishes to have an identity of her own and earnestly seeks it :

> ...I met a man, loved him. Call
> Him not by any name, he is everyman
> Who wants a woman, just as I am every
> Woman who seeks love. In him...the hungry haste
> Of rivers, in me...the oceans' tireless
> Waiting. Who are you, I ask each and everyone,
> The answer is, it is I. Anywhere and,
> Everywhere, I see the one who calls himself
> If in this world, he is tightly packed like the
> Sword in its sheath. It is I who drink lonely
> Drinks at twelve, midnight, in hotels of strange towns,
> It is I who laugh, it is I who make love

> And then, feel shame, it is I who lie dying
> With a rattle in my throat. I am sinner,
> I am saint, I am the beloved and the
> Betrayed. I have no joys which are not yours, no
> Aches which are not yours. I too call myself I.
>
> ("An Introduction," 43-59)

The concluding section of the poem brings to the surface the problematic of a woman's identity, the male identity is everywhere taken for granted as suggested by the image "the sword in its sheath." The poem ends with the enumeration of unconventional roles a woman is not expected to play by categorizers. But not withstanding moral-socio-political categorization, every woman has a self and the subjective need to call herself "I." In Kamala Das's poems, the quest for identity of a woman as a woman goes a long way in making the self out of various disjunctive psychosomatic pressures which make her sometimes a victim and sometimes a crazy woman in whom we find an evaluating reason. Writing on the motif of isolation in contemporary American women's poetry, Deborah Pope says,

> In modern confessional poetry, as an extension of the Adamic tradition, the stance of Everyman is readily available to the male poet. It is expected that, personally alienated and desperate as his voice may be, it is still the voice of his time. By articulating the personal psychoses of his experience, he is simultaneously relaying the social fabric of his world. Yet, for the female confessional poet, there is not the same extension. She is not Everyman, and is hardly Everywoman. Her experience only serves to reinforce her sense of isolation and freakishness. She cannot even believe in a solidarity or community with other woman. Although in a very real sense male confessional poets do bespeak trauma of their times, poets like Sylvia Plath and Anne Sexton remain individual "crazy women."[4]

But in case of Kamala Das's poems, her experience of isolation, instead of being internalized, surfaces and becomes part of a woman's experience in its macro-cosmic implication in the concluding lines of the poem. This could be seen clearly in the poem "The Looking Glass" in which Kamala Das exhorts women to be cautious in matters of love; it is a poem which suggests that woman's weakness lies in her body, which has its needs.

> Oh yes, getting
> A man to love is easy, but living
> Without him afterwards may have to be
> Faced....
> His last voice calling out your name and your
> Body which once under his touch had glared
> Like burnished brass, now drab and destitute.
>
> ("The Looking Glass," 16-24)

The possibility of living without satisfying its endless hungers is depicted in a sad state. The poem underscores male exploitation. The poem also shows that the female body seems to make her a victim of male domination, which she whole-heartedly resents. The anatomical images found in the poem seem to have their source in her intrinsic dislike of body, which seems to limit the horizon of the self. The anatomical images, free and frank erotic lyricism are part of the creative repertory of Kamala Das as is the case with other women poets. Kamala Das may or may not be serious about women's emancipation from male domination, but as a poet she is seriously and creatively concerned with her own identity as a woman. While exploring the theme of making the self she also explores the possibility of adapting the language of men poets to voice her own feelings as a woman, wife, mother, and citizen.

REFERENCES

1. M.L. Rosenthal and Sally M. Gall. *The Modern Poetic Sequence : The Genesis of Modern Poetry* (New York : OUP, 1983) : 393.
2. Kamala Das. *My Story* (New Delhi : Sterling Publishers, 1976) : 81.
3. Keki N. Daruwalla. "Introduction," *Two Decades of Indian Poetry* : 1960-1980 (Sahidabad : Vikas Publishing House Pvt. Ltd., 1980) : XXVII.
4. Deborah Pope. *A Separate Vision : Isolation in Contemporary Women's Poetry* (Baton Rogers : Lousiana State UP, 1984) : 6-7.

13

The Irony of Sex : The Gloss or the Teakwood (A Study of Kamala Das)

I.K. SHARMA

The greatest gift of the Renaissance in Europe, it is said is the discovery of America. The search for the new, the hunger for the unknown, finally led the Europeans to its shore. The greatest gift of the Indian Renaissance, on the other hand, is the discovery of the self. This Indian adventure in the reverse direction offered a variety of patterns in the long course of its journey. The patterns emerged and disappeared at short intervals. In other words, he new road that opened at the intellectual level in the nineteenth century was traversed by all those who had come in contact with the English language and through it with the Euopean culture. From Derozio to Tagore it ran smooth showing no major ups and downs, no sharp turns along the way. At a later stage, this road forked out in two different directions : the one terminated in the poetry of Sri Aurobindo and the other, after some initial jerks, led to *A Time to Change.*

Anyway, the history of Indian English poetry has been mainly the story of male voice, male imagination, and male strategies. A quick run through Gokak's anthology will illustrate my point. Torus and Sarojinis were few and they were emotional at filial and patriotic levels. Their vertical vision had enough music and colour, strength and affection. But they rarely spoke with their hearts inside out.

The advantage of the discovery of the self on the second branch road threw up a poet that shook all accepted norms of a stable male-oriented society. This poet was Kamala Das. If at present a question is put to a reader, inside the classroom or in the street, why after all he likes the poetry of Kamala Das, the reply in most cases will run on predictable lines : that is, she frankly speaks about her sex life. This callow response tells us that the reader reacts what is in his mind and not what is in the poem. In his admiration for the gloss he misses the teakwood.

Where and how to find the teakwood? An effort may be made to find out where it, in effect, lies. A study of the words frequently employed by the poet may be helpful to reveal, in a measure, the working of her mind. These words should fall under two tables. The first one has an enchanting variety : *marriage, wedding drums, bedroom, bride, bouquet, double-bed, pillow, mirrors, bangles, bells, gems, sandal, scent, musk deals : lipstick, gems, perfumes, oils, breast, flesh, mouth, lips, lick, kiss, embrace, love, lust, honeymoon, hair, pigtails, legs, heart, womb, spittle, pubis,* — the whole world of woman along with her cultural paraphernalia is at our door. But what enchants the reader unsettles the poet.

In search of themes the British poets went out to Italy, France, Germany, Greece, Russia, America and India. But Kamala Das like many modern woman poets does not go that far. Nor does she contrive a fictional world of her own. Instead, she looks to herself and into herself. Her body is her Malgudi. That is her greatest curiosity shop. Also, it is her most intimate and sensitive instrument of judging the *world.* She collects evidence through its responses and chronicles them in her own non-conformist, unhackneyed way. Sometimes she looks back at those responses (body's wisdom) in anger but rarely with satisfaction.

> The tragedy of life
> is not death but *growth*........
>
> This love......Yes,
> It was my desire that made him male
> And beautiful ......

The *growth* she generally hint's at in her poetry is not of virgin into woman but of girl into wife and mother. All along the course of human history we have been used to thinking things from the male point of view — virgin, hymen, etc. But nowhere does

Kamala Das talk of this old stuff. The reason : in her case, the sturdy female vision is pressing hard for recognition.

Her body, as has been pointed out, with numerous sensitive centres all over, taperecords, invisibly, no doubt, the contents of her daily experience. It traps all sensations, all songs, all shifts. It responds to all 'stabs' that love can offer,

I enter other's
Lives, and
Make of every trap of lust
A temporary home.

Woman, is this happiness, this lying buried
Beneath a man?........
The world extends a lot beyond his six-foot frame.

When you leave, I drive my blue battered car
Along the bluer sea. I run up the forty
Noisy steps to knock at another's door.

Put together, her poetry is a dissertation, and that too a well documented one of her lived experiences. And the experiences she has in life as we often come across in her poems, are of an unkind variety.

an armful
Of! sprinters...designed to hurt, and
Pregnant with pain.

She feels 'raped' in life by all — husband, lover, society and also the 'humorous heaven.'

I am wronged, I am wronged,
I am so wronged...

Therefore, whatever experiences she records in her poems are all intimations of isolation and turbulence and not of tranquillity, which many readers may love to hear from her. Her poetry, on this score, has achieved a certain degree of distinction.

Her chief contribution to modern Indian poetry is not only the stunning frankness she betrays in every line she writes (that is her chief distinguishing mark, no doubt), but also in making public a vast fund of agonies and information regarding woman's psychic experience that lay hidden for ages in the private female sector. She throws the 'unholy' sanctum sanctotum open and etches out in all caustic details in full public view. And on that account, she has become, unwittingly though, a female Pope of the brave now woman who can look to her with deference for inspiration, guidance and commitment.

This quick short view of the nature and range of her poetry may go to prove that the words I have listed above in the first category are not in any way unrelated to the area the poet chooses to write about. However, to what use she finally puts those words to is quite a different matter.

On the other hand, the second table of words is of ungenteel character and that may well offend the sophisticated/of many/taste readers. But to understand Kamala Das in proper perspective this vast lexicon, too, should not go unexamined. In fact, it is of immense value to us. The words that lie scattered in her poems are : *bones, skeleton, burning, half-burnt, 'morques, x-ray rooms, dark cavern, tomb, pyre, bier, mire, garbage, burial, corpsebearers, mourners, fire, ash, coal, gutter, black veil, lesbian, hetero, frigid urine, cabaret, poison, eunuchs, convicts, murder, blood-slain, menstrual blood, rabid, schizophrenia, eczema, mildew, arthritis, ischemia anaemia, illness, death, hacking, virus etc.* Even the birds, insects, and animals that flash across her nomadic mind are bizarre. They are : *maggots, white ants, toad (stool), spider, snake, lizard, rats, krauts, cat, crow, goose.* How akin to Robert Browing![1]

Evidently, the two set of words classified above are opposed to each other in their nature, tone, and texture. And a reader who limits himself only to the first list may find her poetry toothsome and flattering, and who, only to the second, brackish and may be brutish. But the use of both sets of words in her poetry is ironical : the first is used to tease and not to titillate, and the second, to drive the hard point home by the method of repulsion. In short, the poetry of Kamala Das lies in the tension that these two sets of words cause and set in motion and the world they eventually evoke. It is their interaction that holds her poems together. Thus, the congress of these two sets of words modifies and affects the meaning in a given poem.

Cleanth Brooks tells us that irony "is not only an

acknowledgement of the pressures of a context. Invulnerability to irony is the stability of a context in which the internal pressures balance and mutually support each other. The stability is like that of the arch : the very forces which are calculated to drag the stones to the ground actually provide the principle of support — a principle in which thrust and counter thrust become the means of stability."[2] But why, after all, does a poet, a modern poet, use irony as his chief weapon? The same critic argues further : "A great deal of modern poetry does use irony as its special and perhaps its characteristic energy. For this there are reasons, and compelling reasons. To cite only a few of these reasons : there is the breakdown of a common symbolism; there is the general scepticism as to universals; not feast important, there is the depletion and corruption of language itself, by advertising and by the mass-produced arts of radio, the moving picture and pulp fiction..... For the modern poet is not addressing simple primitives but a public sophisticated by commercial art."[3]

In the earlier part of the discussion I visualized two kinds of readers : one, who will be taken in by the charming rosary of words (the first list), and two, who may show distaste for the blacklisted words (the second list) and on that account, may even shun her poetry.

Irony "postulates a double audience," observes, Fowler, "consisting of one party that hearing shall hear and shall not understand and another party when more is meant than meets the ear, is aware both of that more and of the outsider's incomprehension."

To find out irony in a poem is in fact a tricky affair. It is not easy to say 'here it lies'; it is to be detected in the lines, in the combination of words, in the literary devices the poet may have employed. Sometimes the reader has to discover for himself the missing links and build his own arches (if the poem is long) along the way, for irony in a work of art, like the mythical river Saraswati may appear here and disappear there, show up again only to get lost in the dunes ahead. The function of a critic, then, should be to discover those unseen points lost for the time being and relate their mutual relevance in the structure of the poem.

Modern poets as has already been pointed out, are given to irony. They do not, in other words, make simple, direct and categorical statements. In their poetry, fair is foul and foul is fair, a Solomon is a clown and a clown, Solomon. They say one thing and may mean another. Their praise may be derision and their derision, praise. All this means that an ironist is a conscious artist practising his art with circumspection. A simple-looking question in a poem may be ironic. Polite addresses in a given context may be ironic. The action of a character in a certain scene may be ironic. The playful use of words in a particular situation may be ironic. Various figures of speech like oxymoron, litotes hyperbole may be ironic depending on the context, and so on. Even a role a poet assigns to himself may be sham, and thus, ironic. In other words, irony is "essentially a social mode of speech, saying and meaning different things to different groups, playing on a differentiation within the audience."[4] A German scholar, too defines irony as that which denotes "the rejection of any kind of 'plain' view of life, of any facile panoramic view and of any view the significance of the individual features of which can be understood."[5]

This foregoing analysis may make us aware of the sources and "ways of irony" in Kamala Das. When she says

It's only
To save my face, I flaunt; at
Times, a grand, flamboyant lust.
(*The Freaks*)

The impression should not be that she has a limitless appetite for sex but read carefully along with the title, the poem may reveal her endless quest for love. The reader should not be taken in just by the posture she adopts. Behind the lines there lurks a figure with a glint of irony in her eyes.

When the poet takes the world "so seriously, experience so deeply its inner contradiction, its mystery that cannot be put into words, that he is no longer able to express himself in ordinary speech; he is forced to use extraordinary means of expression. The great irony of the Romantics, as well as of Socrates is of this kind."[6]

. . . . oh, never mind, I've
spent long years trying to locate my mind

Beneath skin, beneath flesh and underneath
The bone.

But at the same time the poetry of Kamala Das does not take a reader to the "dream level; which the poetry of Romantics often does nor does it catapult him to the 'blissful mainland' showing him a variegated cloud bank" on the way which the Socratic irony may do. However, one thing is evident that Kamala Das rejects the super-celestial world and struggles to find everything — ideal love, lover, and herself — here and now. And in case she fails to get any of them and which is often the case, she lets out her stream build up in isolation in her poetry.

Yes,
I sang solo, my songs were lonely, but they did
Echo beyond the world's unlighted edge.

Her mode of stating simple facts of life is ironic. Apparently a statement may appear innocuous but in the given context it changes the poem with a new meaning. A small poem like *The Fancy-Dress* may be analysed, for example. Right from the start, the tone of the poet is noticeable,

Every virtue requires today
A fancy dress.

Then the poet slowly builds up through common words, her attack on the priest, the politician, the patriots, who have ignored 'the children of the poor.' They (the poor) now lie unclaimed in the city morgues. And, therefore, in the end, the passing kick :

God is in His heaven and all
Is right with this *stinking world.*

One word 'stinking' used here is enough to open new worlds of association, from the God of Browning to the gods of India. In the context, the real meaning lies behind the apparent meaning. What is 'intended' is 'pretended.'

Another poem *An Apology To Goutama* is not an invocation which the name of 'Goutama' may suggest but a sly rejection of his hand because

While your arms hold

My-woman-form, his hurting arms
Hold my very soul.

An ironic way to deflate the religious pride of man.

But the two poems I have referred to above are not 'sexy' in nature as poems like, *In love*, *The Freaks*, *The Stone Age*, *The Looking Glass*, *Convicts*, *The Conflagration*, *The Doubt*, *The Invitation*, *Substitute*, *The Old Playhouse*, *Gino*, etc., are. They have the slices of sex in them, floating.

To be brief, the chief sources of her poetry are : her child-memory, her eyes (I mean, what they see around : social reality), and her body. I did not discuss the first two in the earlier section of this paper, nor do I propose to do it now except making a passing reference to them. Her recalling the past has an ironic glint if seen in the context of the poems where it occurs. Very often it is noted she leaps heavily on her memory (and her grandmother and her old house come alive) and from thereon she leaps on to a new subject in the poem. Thus, the past she recounts may be seen as a symbol of old human ties. Placed alongside the present where she is searching for love, the past recalled throws right on the contemporary values.

Secondly, there are a few poems like, *The Dance of the Eunuchs* that reveal her remarkable power of observation. It is one of those poems where she has not made use of the first person pronoun; otherwise there is God's plenty in her poetry. And significantly, she succeeds in retaining the artistic control and distance a great deal. The irony in it springs up by 'contrast,' which she has so deftly carried out through the poem. Other poems like, *Lines Addressed To a Devadasi* and *Death of the Goat*, too, are free from the ubiquitious 'I' and they too click, though at a different level. *The irony of divergence*, which according to Green opens up an unexpected dimension which adds to our understanding of the original statement is noticeable in some of these poems, and others.

Her 'body' poems, lastly, have attracted a wider readership for their lyrical directness, immediacy, and quickness. They have in them all that the female sensibility can undisguisedly offer. Through these poems she defines and redefines her self — her shifting moods, her amatory experiences in a world peopled by fond husband ... old fat spider and his ilk. In doing so she seems to be in a hurry to let out the feelings of the moment go on paper. Hence, her body poems have become the honest vernacular of her heart.

But behind them all, there sits an ironist who looks at this pachydermous world with her characteristic cynicism. Her tone, by turn, goes sentimental and sardonic as that of Jules Laforgue. Her poems *A Request* and *Lines to a Husband* can be cited as illustrations.

When I die
Do not throw the meat and bones away
But pile them up
And
Let them tell
By their smell
What life was worth
On this earth
What love was worth
In the end. (*A Request*)

And here is the opening stanza of *The Impossible* by the French poet.

Tonight I may die. Rain, wind, sun
Will scatter everywhere my heart, my nerves, my marrow.
All will be over for me. Neither deep not awakening.
I shall not have been there among the stars.

How close they are to each other in thought, style and tone. The most notable feature of her irony, in the end, is that it does not send the reader to 'a wild elephant chase' (a case of unstable irony) but retains him, all along, in the region where "Once a reconstruction of meaning has been made, the reader is not then invited to undermine it with further demolitions and reconstructions" (A case of 'stable' Irony).

To sum up, a close reading of the whole corpus of Kamala Das's poetry reveals the tone of the poet all through is 'nihilistic and corrosive' which modern poetry so abundantly offers. The theme of sex which she generally throws up ('the cheapest bait') is only a gilt-edged device to pin down the reader. From there she takes him to a 'higher meaning' by offering evidence after evidence of that inside the body of the poem. But to know that evidence the reader (if he is initiated, well and good) has to work a little.

Otherwise, he, will miss much of the charm of her poetry and will not be able to differentiate between the gloss and the teakwood.

NOTES AND REFERENCES

1. James Reeves in *Commitment To Poetry* says that Robert Browning had "a taste for keeping strange pets, which persisted all his life. Among the animals he encouraged were — *toads, spiders, lizards, a bat,* and *two geese;*" 158.

2. Cleanth Brooks. "Irony as a Principle of Structure," in *Twentieth Century Criticism,* The Major Statements, ed. William J. Handy Max Westbook; 62.

3. Brooks 67.

4. D.H. Green. *Irony in the Medieval Romance* (OUP, 1979) : 367.

5. Max Brod. *Heinrich Heine,* tr. by Joseph Witriol (London, 1956) : 201.

6. Brod 209.

14

Treatment of Nature in Kamala Das's Poetry

C.C. VARKEY*

The studies of Commonwealth Literature adequately reveal that they deal with the Literatures of the countries once ruled or colonised by the British, thus introducing and analysing the influence of colonialism in literature. Commonwealth Literature, either colonial or post-colonial, has in no way been impeded or stinted, retarded or retrogressed in its creative expression by the use of English as a vehicle. Perhaps, the English language, the common and uniform legacy of all the Commonwealth Literatures, has served as a catalyst and synthesiser to exhilerate, invigorate and accelerate the creative consciousness, resulting in the general expression of Commonwealth consciousness. While the English language stood accommodating socially, culturally, historically and linguistically to the varying needs of the complex Commonwealth creativity, it also paved the way for the articulation of various aspects of literature, such as aesthetic, nostalgic, geographic, naturalistic, ethnic and so on.

Unlike the literature of West Africa that offers the most passionate expression of the colonial confrontation with an intensity unique in aesthetic formulation of form and feeling, or the Canadian scene that presents a more complicated fabric of divisions and diversities, or the New Zealandian situation that gives rise to a

*Lecturer (Sl. Grade), Research Centre, Department of English, St. Thomas College, Trichur.

sharpness in thought and feeling in literature trying to confront the realities of dismantling prejudices, illusions and arrogance in an aesthetic understanding of colonial situation, the impact of colonial encounter does not seem to have appeared very sharp on Indian scenario. The most the colonial encounter has done is to turn the Indian consciousness upon its own socio-cultural ills and drawbacks. Two very clear patterns of expression emerged from its constructs. One, of unified fervour, passion and devotion to one's own country and culture and the second, of dissipated withdrawal in criticism, search for identity and conflict between self and society. The dominant tone of voice in the pioneers like Sri Aurobindo and Tagore was one of philosophical nationalism. The chief assertions of the nationalistic fervour in their creative works were either revivalistic or visionary. Subsequently, it became the destiny of Indian literature in English to be influenced more by personalities than by politics. Kamala Das, their true successor, is not an exception to the tends set by them.

Kamala Das has often been labelled as a confessional poet and indeed in tone and structure her poetry may be called 'autobiographical.' But many critics and readers fail to comprehend the fact that a poet often invents facts and experiences fictionalising them as 'real and authentic' to achieve the reader's total participation. It is true that Kamala Das expresses her need for love, a sense of urgency and fulfilment with a frankness and naiveness unusual in the Indian context. However, a rigid and unrelenting categorization of her poems into inflexible train of thoughts and attitudes is to adversely affect the imaginative dimensions of their appreciation. Apart from the poignant and easily tangible aspects of her poetry, some of the minor, yet significant, features are left unnoticed by her critics as well as her enthusiasts. It is very interesting to examine her poetry from a new angle of appreciation hitherto hardly ever attempted, namely, her treatment of nature and landscape in her poems.

Some of her earliest creations are a case in point. 'A Hot Noon in Malabar' and 'My Grandmother's House' are laden with nostalgia and yearning for what cannot be retrieved. At the same time, her fond recreation of the past gives new pathos and better sensibility to her present life. Nalapat house, her ancestral home, picturised as an old, but proud edifice with the lustrous, haunting presence of her beloved grandmother has withdrawn into silence with only the snakes sometimes to disturb the silence of the books. The grandmother and the house are living entities to the poet's mind, bringing into her the antique, but unravished majesty and magnificence of the surrounding scenes. The acute sense of the loss of the abundant warmth and love is woven into the intensity of the localised picture of the 'blind eyes of windows,' 'the frozen air' and the sombre, weird, discarded house. Local colouration and scenic splendour reign the entire poem 'A Hot Noon in Malabar.' Every microscopic image provides expositions in an ascending scale of complexities drawn from the simple confrontation of the self with the landscape in varying dimensions. In this poem every minute detail of the 'hot noon' portrays triumphant struggle of the poet to resolve herself in identification with 'the beggars with whining voices,' 'men who come from hills with parrots in a cage and fortune cards,' 'brown Kurava girls with old eyes,' 'bangle-sellers who spread on the cool black floor those red and green and blue bangles.' Each species of the delineated portraits carry with its person peculiar characteristics of its locale. The entire landscape transcends from its earthly, barren hollowness to a higher realm of transfigured uniqueness and wholeness. The poet's communion with the inextricably knit images in the poem dissolves her identity into each of them to transform into an impersonated spectre of scenic beauty. Here the landscape and history of Malabar offer a mixture of exotic splendour to the scintillating 'hot noon.' The judicious juxtaposition of light and shadow, song and noise, dust and grating, strangers and mistrust mutually and contrastingly affords for the 'wildness' of the scene along with 'wildmen, wild thoughts, wild love.' The poet's earnest craving for deliverance from the inner crisis of wildness and domesticity, rurality and urbanity, uncouthness and sophistication is aptly corresponding to the complicated 'natural' situation in which the characters are pictured in the poem.

In 'The Freaks' the poet selects grotesque and bizarre metaphors from nature. Associating human situation with elements from nature is admirably wrought through the symbols of 'sun-stained cheek,' 'his mouth, a dark cavern, where stalactites of uneven teeth gleam,' 'the puddles of desire' and 'coiling snakes of silence.' The general criticism that in a crazy bid to give vent to intense emotion, Indian creativity suffers lack of suggestiveness is adequately challenged by the aforesaid illustrations. The structural framework of the poem falls in unlaboured harmony with the images from elemental forces in 'The Sunshine Cat' as in 'The Freaks.' The widening or the waning sun aggravates or dwindles the 'Cat' in the woman 'locked in a room of books.' Here 'the cat' is the symbol of unleashed creative fire between resurrection and crucifixion neither of which she can appropriate fully. 'The sunshine (cat)' — that life-sustaining ethos — only parched her tongue and scorched her passion till 'she was cold and half-dead.' The irreparable ravages that the 'cynics' whose chests had 'new hair sprouted like great-winged moths,' inflicted upon her physical passion with 'their young lusts,' remained in her as an indelible mark of her unquenched urge. Here is the nature that ravishes her, but does not give her fulfilment; altogether it is a grotesque experience for the protagonist in the poem.

'The Invitation' and 'Advice To Fellow Swimmers' present diametrically opposed images of one of the powerful elements of nature — the sea. Though the sea is not a recurring theme in Kamala Das's poetry, its forceful impact on her transports her into philosophical speculations of existential and ascetic nature of life, negation of life, death and universal life. In 'The Invitation' the 'garrulous sea' offers a kind of death, a complete negation. The disintegration of the body into the vital forces of nature is a gain to the sea; at the same time it is not a loss to the invited one since it saves the body from 'a funeral pyre with a burning head.' Moreover, it is a metamorphosis and not mortality that the sea invites her to embrace. Both the invitations, one by the sea and the other by her lover, means death, the former a complete negation and the latter a metaphorical death. The outstretched lap of the sea offers her limbs 'cool secret sands' to relax and 'anemones' to pillow her head. The poet finally releases herself from the tantalising situation by choosing death 'on beds,' 'limbs inert,' 'cells expanding into throbbing suns.' Her refusal to the sea's invitation makes here more intensely conscious of her precarious ontological existence as she cannot escape from the 'prying' of the sea. More fantastic and fascinating is the picture of the revitalising fish coming up frequently for air. It seems that the repeatedly emerging fish is in constant conspiracy with the prying sea in intruding into her privacy. One cannot be a ceaseless holocaust to one's own selfish self. The ultimate aim is to cross one's own body, 'the familiar pest,' so as to sink identity into the oceanic universe. Thus, in 'Advice To Fellow Swimmers,' as well as in the other poem, the poet presents the soul of the sea and the sea of the soul, the soul in the sea and the sea in the soul. The sea's ever widening horizon renders abiding asylum to the wandering spirits with therapeutic treatment. The seeming semblance of the sea as a destructive force in 'The Invitation,' and the cosmic soul of the sea as a redemptive force in 'Advice To Fellow Swimmers' are only the two forces of the same nature yielding only to a sublime consciousness.

'Nani' rises to the realm of mythification and apotheosis to the children who witnessed the 'clumsy puppet' hanging in the privy, after the shrubs had overgrown the entire premise making the abandoned privy 'an altar then, a lonely shrine' for the sacrificial victim. The lurid spectacle of Nani hanging from the rope arouses not so much horror as the spectacled stare of the arid grandmother clinging on to a stringent set of conventional, obsolete moral code. The 'Tharavadu' with its antique, inscrutable, impregnable mystery remains as a haunting monument and silent spectator to the uncanny existence of the perversions and exploitations in a puritan society. The entire gamut of the poem 'My son's teacher's tragedy is pathetic and painful. The colourful picture of the long, gaudy procession of the devotees carrying 'pink elephant gods,' clapping cymbals, beating drums and singing aloud only accentuates the bitter predicament of the teacher, lying swooned on a grey pavement with her new skirt flapping and fluttering like a green flag flying at half mast. The irrevocable symbol of death reigns both the pictures. The solemn procession heralds the death of the god while the wind-blown skirt proclaims the teacher's death.

In 'Middle Age' and in 'Punishment in Kintergarten,' a succession of endless images cram the scenic situation with delicate touch and tender feelings. Middle age is a time for one to reminisce wistfully about 'a time of the squirrels' invitation to their jungle feast, writing in golden ink and posting it at night. The child's punishment in Kintergarten takes a new dimension with minute and meticulous descriptions when the blue-frocked woman drains 'the honey-coloured day of peace' with her words throwing at the child like pots and pans. The child's aching communion with 'the steel-white sun' when she buries her face 'in the sun-warmed hedge and smells the flowers and pain,' is consoling and compensating for the acute loneliness of both the child and the sun. The sun's solicitude for the child extends its all embracing arm to shield the child from its solitude.

This post-colonial creative subject is self-conscious, sufficiently enough, to turn to oneself, in order to examine the extent of boundary in which she can move about in a 'room of one's own.' To Kamala Das, nationality is not a post-modern suspect, nor is it a narrow, selfish, narcissistic room of the male where woman has no voice. It is a vast landscape with immense possibilities rendered so with a poetic search for identity and conflict between self and society. Assertion of personality is indeed a major distinguishable feature of post-colonial literature. But the confessional dimension of Kamala Das's poetry reaches for the universal in the reader's total participation in the writer's textualization/fictionalization of such vital experiences as nature and landscape in her poems.

As far as the Indian scene is concerned, its oddity and individuality as evidenced in its creativity in the vast spectrum of Commonwealth Literature is amply represented by the poetry of Kamala Das. The contradictions within the Indian ethos, ideology, culture, history, language and aesthetics, have provided Kamala Das with sufficient creative provocation rendering her poems indigenous as well as making it a partaking in the angst, generally felt in the Commonwealth Literature. Thus, the nativised network of her poetry renders it a better globalised glow than the so-called global literature.

REFERENCES

1. Paranjape, Makarand (ed.), 1993. *Indian Poetry in English*. Madras : Macmillan India Limited.
2. Rama Murti, K.S. (ed.), 1995. *Twentyfive Indian Poets in English.* Madras : Macmillan India Limited.
3. Dr. A.N. Kapoor (ed.), 1979. *Indo-Anglican Poetry.* Allahabad : Kitab Mahal.

15

Kamala Das — Need for Re-assessment

SHARAD RAJIMWALE*

Ms. Kamala Das has mostly been assessed as a writer in the genre of confessional poetry. She has been ranked with such poetesses of dissatisfaction and discontent as Sylvia Plath and Anne Sexton, though the comparison is seen by many as undeserving.

There are essentially two sides to Ms. Das's poetry; one is that which is extraordinarily centred around her own self, probing the malaise and morbidity that seem to clamp on her poetic vision. Over the years, it is this side that has been turned to our view, and she has been dismissed and rated accordingly.

> Why not leave
> Me alone, critics, friends, visiting cousins,
> Every one of you? Why not let me speak in
> Any language I like?

Things that came from her pen was something new, as no woman writer had ever before written with such power and honesty. The other side emerges from this, or seen from another angle, is a dimension of it. Her poetry constitutes not just a compelling expression of personal experiences and a forceful subjective voice, but more importantly, a phenomenon unlike any other in Indian English poetry. She is the first woman poet to crack the mould, and establish an attitude and viewpoint the Indian readers were quite unfamiliar with.

---

*Lecturer, Department of English, Gulbarga University, Gulbarga.

I wore a shirt and my Brother's trousers,
cut my hair short and ignored My womanliness.

Readers whose tastes and expectations were formed by compositions like 'Morning Serenade,' 'Our Casuarina Tree,' 'The Queen's Rival,' 'Caprice,' 'The Lady of the Night' and such like, were shocked and staggered, by what Kamala Das wrote. It was so unconventional, so hurtfully new, so outrageously anti-traditional. What the general readers reacted to immediately was the bold and frank confessional tone she wrote in and broad imagery seeking to convey the hurts and humiliations she received in her personal life. It is true that personal voice is very strong in her, and from one point of view it provides a very limited scope. However, this voice is so strong that it extends beyond the personal world of anguished feelings and assumes wider significance.

I am sinner,
I am saint. I am the beloved and the
Betrayed. I have no joys which are not yours,
No aches which are not yours,
I too call myself I

There is a strange power in the way she conveys meaning through concrete imagery which have pictorial vividness, tactile immediacy, and auditory impact. The areas of experience these images reveal have long lain submerged; it required unusual courage to bring them to light. A profoundly restless spirit fired by the "passional force," to use D.H. Lawrence's expression, that originates in a mind that sees and hears and is aware of a disharmonious life, of the hurt inflicted by coercive subjugation and complete obliteration of the self, needed a new idiom, a new repertoire of images and symbols and a new poetic approach, the conventional being woefully inadequate. One easily discerns ruggedness in her metre, savagery in her images, a complete denial of all that the Toru Dutt — Sarojini Naidu — Nilima Devi tradition stood for.

'Sleek crows flying/like poison on wing,' 'a meagre rain that smelt of dust in/Attics and the urine of lizards and mice,' 'The city morgues are full of unclaimed cadavers,' 'You heard the sparrows in gutters,' 'I am moved by fancies that are curled/Around these images, and cling.'

Such expressions, and they come so naturally, so forcefully, cannot be dismissed as expressions of a fevered mind or a warped personality verging on nymphomaniac tendencies, as has usually been done. They are different tones and pitches of a voice articulating her deep mistrust of the conventional.

The conventional modes in Indian English poetry have been unable to convey reality, rather they have only glossed it over. Kamala Das confronts reality in its brutal and ugliest forms. Her poetic techniques and language coalesce with her mood and with her experience content.

> I who have lost my way and beg now at stranger's
> doors to Receive love, at least in small change?

Her most notable strength lies in confronting the reality of her experiences which in poem after poem becomes symptomatic of the general suffering of countless women. As Ms. Margaret Dickie observes in a different context,

> '... if the voices of women are not mute, neither are they the voice of the dominant culture. They are rather new voices at the fringes of society, where language changes and develops, Woman's poetry has always been a channel for such voices."

What Sylvia Plath, Adrienne Rich, Judith Wright, Margaret Atwood, Anne Sexton, Phyllis Webb, Margaret Avison, Rosemary Sullivan and Susan Griffins are doing in British, American, Canadian and Australian poetry was begun by Kamala Das in Indian English poetry. These woman poet's gesture of defiance and self-assertion snowballed into a movement first and later on a genre. It took a Kamala Das here to say without mincing words,

> I am not yours for asking
> Not because of morality
> but because
> I don't feel the need.

She was joined after a few hesitations by Mamta Kalia, Eunice de Souza, Margaret Chatterjee, Sunita Namjoshi, Gauri Deshpande and a whole generation of younger poetesses to establish an image of woman totally unencumbered by the conventional falsifying colours. This was not a personal matter but a whole generation's pangs of birth, not an individualistic attitudinizing but a painful transformation coming over feminine consciousness.

> "To fight for the dignity and true emancipation of women is the most difficult task especially because it involves values and attitudes that are deep-rooted not only in the minds of men but also in the consciousness of women.... The period of transition manifests contradictory patterns, the subjugation and the emergence of new forms of bondage and subjugation in the new era of dominance of money and market.... The concept of freedom of women in practice is grossly vulgarized throwing up extremely grotesque and distorted forms of 'freedom' in a "transitional society combining the worst of both worlds."

Kamala Das's poetry embodies agonies of women emerging from that state of subjugation and bondage, and seeking to establish their identity and the self. Obviously, this is not an easy and uncomplicated process, as this involves discarding a lot, adopting a defiant attitude and probing the bruised self that expresses itself in so many different moods ranging from despair and dejection to anger and bewildered sense of rootlessness. This is best expressed through felt emotions in an intensely personalised idiom. It is easy enough to see in such a stance a dislocated mind suffering the nightmares of a shut-in life devastated and laid bare by a hyper-sexed, self-willed and schizophrenic woman. This is precisely what prevailing critical attitude to her poems highlights, which is not only lamentably lop-sided, but indicative of an alarmingly impoverished angle of critical outlook in Indian English Criticism. In a vein which issues from this dominant critical approach, her poems are seen as the expression of the pitiable plight of a defenceless woman who needs love, consideration and sympathy and desires a loving husband, warmth and home.

Such an interpretation comes from a reluctance to give up the traditional mental attitude, for what is more heartwarming than the return of the defiant woman to the conventional age-old mould of the 'categorizers'? It misses the basic point about her poetry; it is essentially a poetry of protest, of defiance and of emphatic assertion, all other moods ranging from weak feminine sense of helplessness and submission, to a restless search for happiness and shelter are different expressions of this basic Promethean spirit which is eager to break the rusted shackles and have its voice heard.

> As the convict studies
> His prison's geography
> I study the trappings
> of your body, dear love,
> For I must someday find
> An escape from its snare

Whether she explores her sexual experiences and encounters or the seamy side of public life, cities, dwellings, and streets — there can always be noted the defiant, ironical tone in her poetry. No other Indian English poet employed irony to such devastating effect before Kamala Das — it is caustic, it is Virgilian, it is profoundly demolishing. It evokes both pity and anger, sympathy and ire.

Kamala Das's poetry presents Indian woman in a way that has outraged the usual male sense of decency and decorum. Kamala Das inaugurates a new age for woman poets by doing so, an age seeking to forge new idiom, a new medium and newer modes of address, constituting a total rejection of the conventional modes of poetic expression of the dominant culture. The shock generated by this is something resembling the shock created by the experimental poets of the 1920s (Hulme, Pound and Eliot) who decided that the time had come to liberate English poetry from the Georgian decadence and rejuvenate it. Though no such high claims can be made for Kamala Das, her importance as an inaugurator of a new poetic awareness for Indian woman poets is an established fact. As a critic has observed, "She deals with the conflict between passivity and rebellion against the male-oriented universe. Her poetry is the acknowledgement and celebration of the beauty and courage of being a woman."

Her medium is a passionate inflamed assertion of that being which has remained mute, suppressed and battered through nameless centuries.

"The central problem in poetry is always the problem of reality, less on the social and more on the psycho-spiritual plain. The existential conditions impinge intensely on the female psyche. The acceptance or rejection, denial or disapproval at the emotional level, whether in love or death creates in her inner storm, a mutiny within," says Elizabeth Smart.

When Kamala Das writes,

> Of what does the burning mouth
> Of sun, burning in today's
> Sky remind me ... Oh, yes, his
> Mouth and ... his limbs like pale and
> carnivorous plants reaching
> Out for me ...

She is not celebrating unbridled sensuality, but projecting the stereotype of a wronged woman and at once asserting the need to establish her voice and identity. As some one observed, we see in her "the calm centre of the storm, the triumphant surge of affirmative projection that comes with a clear perception of despair by an energetically creative spirit."

Those who naively condemn her for her unpretentious frankness and bold portrayal of the living fabric of the passional man-woman relationship defaced and distorted by aberrations coming from socially — culturally determined attitudes, fail to see the basic force and drift of her poetry. Alicia Ostriker, a contemporary critic says :

> "The belief that true poetry is genderless — which is a disguised form of believing that true poetry is masculine — means that we have not learned to see women poets generically, to recognise the tradition they belong to ...."

With Kamala Das it is essentially a matter of attuning our critical vision to "the hidden vistas" of her inner world which has so much to offer to our perturbed, questioning minds. For her poetry is not "a continual self-sacrifice, a continual extinction of personality." As she says in *My Story* "A poet's raw material is not clay or stone; it is her personality. I could not escape from personality." And again,

> "One's real world is not what is outside him. It is the immeasurable world inside him that is real. Only

> the one who has decided to travel inwards, will realize that his route has no end."

Only, Kamala Das's inner world has not remained her personal demesne, it has acquired profound symbolic significance for all bruised and battered womankind.

REFERENCES

1. 'The Alien in Contemporary American Women's Poetry' — Margaret Dickie/ *Contemporary Literature*/Wisconsin University/XXVIII, 3, 1987.
2. *Women in Indian Society,* ed. Rehana Ghadially, Sage Pub., 1988.
3. *Kamala Das* by Devendra Kohli. New Delhi : Arnold-Heinemann, 1974.
4. Quoted by Manorama B. Trikha in 'Contemporary Canadian Poetry by women : a Cosmos of Miscellany," *Meerut Journal of Comparative Literature and Language,* special no. Canadian studies — Vol. V, No. 1, 1992.
5. Kamala Das : Devendra Kohli, N.D. : Arnold-Heinemann, 1974.
6. "Skating the Language : The Emergence of Women's Poetry in America," *Contemporary Literature,* Wisconsin University, 29.2, Summer 1988.
7. *Selected Essays,* T.S. Eliot. Penguin, London.
8. *My Story*, by Kamala Das.

Bibliography

PRIMARY SOURCES

Novels

Alphabet of Lust. New Delhi : Orient Paperbacks, 1976.

Daughter of Immortality. New Delhi : S. Chand & Co., 1985.

Short Stories

A Doll for the Child Prostitute. New Delhi : Indian Paperbacks, 1977.

Padmavathi. The Harlot and Other Stories. New Delhi : Sterling Publishers, 1992.

Sandal Tree and Other Stories. Hyderabad : Disha Books, 1995.

Non-Fiction

My Story : An Autobiography : New Delhi : Sterling Publishers, 1971.

Interviews

Geetha, T.N. "An Interview with Kamala Das." *Indian Women Novelists.* Ed. Dhawan. New Delhi : Prestige Books, 1995. Set II. Vol. 1. 93. ref. : 257.

SECONDARY SOURCES : CRITICAL WORKS

Books

Kaur, Iqbal. *Unitying and Retying the Text : An Analysis of Kamala Das's My Story.* New Delhi : Bahri Publications, 1990.

——. ed. *Perspectives on Kamala Das's Fiction.* New Delhi : Intellectual Book Corner, 1995.

Radha K. *Kamala Das.* Kerala Writers Series. Madras : Macmillan, 1987.

Research Articles

Ahmed, Shafiuddin and Angela Gaewel. "The Politics of Money : Incomplete Feminism in *A Doll's House.*" *Dalhousie Review* 70.2 (1992) : 170-190.

Chandra, Subhash. "A Feminist Reading of *My Story.*" Dhawan, *Indian Women Novelists* Set II. Vol. 1. 141-149.

Dwivedi, A.N. "Kamala Das's *Alphabet of Lust.*" Dwivedi, *Indian Writing in English* 118-125.

Elias, Mohmed. "Kamala Das and the Nayar Heritage." *Journal of Indian Writing in English* 6.2 (1978) : 15-24.

——. "The Short Stories of Kamala Das." *World Literature Written in English* 52.2 (1985) : 307-312. Rpt. in Rajan, *Changing Traditions* 30-37.

Geetha, T.N. "A Study of the Short Stories of Kamala Das." Dhawan, *Indian Women Novelist* Set II. Vol. 1. 175-195.

Harish, Ranjana. "My Story." Jain, *Women's Writing* 213-222.

Kanwadkar, M.M. "Motherly Sensibility in *My Story.*" Dhawan, *Indian Women Novelists* Set II. Vol. 1. 149-155.

Kaur, Iqbal. "Sexual Politics and Kamala Das." Dhawan, *Indian Women Novelists* Set II. Vol. 1. 102-140.

——. "Colonial Anguish in *My Story.*" Dhawan, *Indian Women Novelists* Set II. Vol. 1. 156-169.

——. "Protest Against Sexual Colonialism : Kamala Das's *My Story.*" Jain, *Women Writing* 223-232.

Memon, I.U. "Amrita Pritam's *The Revenue Stamp* and Kamala Das's *My Story.*" Dhawan, *Indian Women Novelists* Set III. Vol. 4.

Lall, Rama Rani. "Rebellion and Escape : Kamala Das's *My Story.*" Jain, *Women's Writing* 233-242.

Narayan, Shyamala A. "A Note on Kamala Das's *My Story.*" *Commonwealth Quarterly* 3.9 (Dec. 1978) : 148-155. Also in Dhawan, *Indian Women Novelists* Set II. Vol. 4. 170-174.

Rahman, Anisur. "A Poet's Tale : *A Doll for the Child Prostitute.*" Prasad, Hari Mohan, *Response* 274–284.

Radha, K. "Common Ground Between the Poems of Kamala Das and Her Other Works in English." *ACLALS Bulletin* 6-7 Ser. 1986.

——. "The Short Stories of Kamala Das. An Analysis." Dhawan, *Indian Women Novelists* Set II. Vol. 1. 191-203.

Shrivastava, K.C. "The Novels of Kamala Das : The Quest for Identity." Sinha and Sinha 117–122. ref. : 519. Rpt. in Dhawan, *Indian Women Novelists* Set II. Vol. 1. 94-101.

——. "Political Spectrum in Kamala Das's *Alphabet of Lust.*" Saxena, *Glimpses* Vol. 1. 124–130.

Uma, Alladi. "What is in a Genre? Kamala Das's *My Story.*" *Literary Criterion* 32.3 (1996) : 69-76.

Usha, V.T. "Literary Paradigms of Matriliny : Kamala Das's *My Story.*" *New Quest* 118, 1990 : 217-220.